A CELEBRATION OF RECIPES FROM THE HEART

The Canadian
HERITAGE
COOKBOOK

Edna McCann

Prentice Hall Canada Inc.
Scarborough, Ontario

Canadian Cataloguing in Publication Data

McCann, Edna
  The Canadian heritage cookbook

ISBN 0-13-573486-X

1. Cookery, Canadian. I. Title.
TX715.6.M33 1996 641.5971 C96-930540-0

 © 1996 Prentice-Hall Canada Inc., Scarborough, Ontario
A Viacom Company

Prentice-Hall, Inc., Englewood Cliffs, New Jersey
Prentice-Hall International (UK) Limited, London
Prentice-Hall of Australia, Pty. Limited, Sydney
Prentice-Hall Hispanoamericana, S.A., Mexico City
Prentice-Hall of India Private Limited, New Delhi
Prentice-Hall of Japan, Inc., Tokyo
Simon & Schuster Asia Private Limited, Singapore
Editora Prentice-Hall do Brasil, Ltda., Rio de Janeiro

ISBN 0-13-573486-X

Acquisitions Editor: Sara Borins
Production Editor: Kelly Dickson
Copy Editor: Tanya Long
Production Coordinator: Julie Preston
Cover and Interior Design: Julia Hall
Page Layout: BJ Weckerle

1 2 3 4 5   00 99 98 97 96

Printed and bound in Canada

Credits:
Cover image courtesy of Saskatchewan Archives Board, R-A23721
January photo courtesy of Archives of Ontario, C 119-1-0-0-5
Page 3: Reprinted with permission of the Estate of Melville Cane.
Page 119: Reprinted with the permission of Simon & Schuster from THE COLLECTED POEMS OF ROBERT P. TRISTRAM COFFIN, New and Enlarged Edition. Copyright © 1948 by Robert P. Tristram Coffin, Renewed 1976 by Margaret Coffin Halvosa.

Table of Contents

Introduction

January

February

March

April

Baked Virginia Ham with Madeira Gravy – 50
Scalloped Potatoes – 51
Fiddleheads with Lemon Butter – 52
Old-Fashioned Scrap Soup – 53
Butter Corn Sticks – 54
Baked Bean and Apple Casserole – 55
Quiche Lorraine – 56
Orange French Toast – 57
Orange Syrup – 57
Southern Chicken Salad – 58
Mustard Dressing – 58
Hearts of Palm Salad – 59
Yogurt Lemon Nut Cake – 59

May

Mother McCann's Rhubarb and Raspberry Jam – 64
Rhubarb Punch – 65
Rhubarb Pie – 66
Pasta Primavera – 67
Pineapple Chicken and Rice Bake – 68
Beef and Sausage Lasagna – 71
Barbequed Back Ribs – 72
Barbequed Fish Fillets – 73
Mixed Fruit – 73
Russian Tea – 74

June

Chocolate Denver Pudding – 78
Dandelion Salad with Pine Nuts – 80
Asparagus with Maltaise Sauce – 81
Asparagus Amandine – 82
Strawberry Ice Cream – 83
Strawberry Custard – 83
Strawberry Shortcake – 85
Baking Powder Biscuits – 85
Grandmother MacIntosh's Potato Salad – 87
Fried Chicken – 88
Tortière – 89
Chicken with Roquefort Cheese – 90

Introduction

W hen I received a call from one of the editors who works on *The Heritage Book* asking if I would be interested in producing a cookbook, I was extremely flattered. I was also very surprised! Although I have included a number of family recipes in *The Heritage Book* over the past several years, I didn't realize that so many of my readers would respond with such enthusiasm to them.

"My grandmother used to make those cookies. I had lost the recipe—thank you!"

"I tried your recipe for the potato casserole. It was delicious!"

From the time I was a very young child when I would help my mother with the baking for the church socials and teas, I have loved baking, cooking and trying all manner of interesting or unusual culinary treats.

As in most families, we have recipes that are particular favourites. These are on the pages in the cookbooks or on cards in the recipe box that are easily identified as the most popular—they are so fingerprinted or splattered with spills that they are barely readable.

I am very pleased and proud to share these recipes with you. Some are old, some new. Many have been handed down from one generation to another with ingredients added or left out as tastes have changed.

I hope that you and your families will enjoy trying all of these recipes. Perhaps they will bring back memories or create new ones for you.

Ready for a vigorous game of ice hockey.

January

Winter—cold is the night.
Chiseled in deepest blue,
Each star-shape silver white
Shines cold—clear down the sky's long avenue.

—Melville Cane

I like to have an early snowfall that stays with us through the winter. This blanket of white is so much more beautiful than a grey-bare landscape. Another winter marvel is the heavy ice storm once called by Mark Twain "nature's most beautiful spectacle." Most of us, however, would rather do without the beauty of such a storm that can cause great damage to trees and bushes and wreak havoc on the highways.

Several years ago I was with friends when a freezing rain storm struck unexpectedly. We were travelling by car and were within about 60 miles of home. Jim, a good and confident driver, felt that we would be able to make it home safely if he reduced his speed and drove cautiously.

As the storm worsened we slowed more and more until we were moving at a snail's pace. Even as we crawled along we passed many cars in the ditch or in the median. After almost three nerve-wracking hours we were within two blocks of home when a strong gust of wind simply blew the car sideways into the ditch.

"Well, we could walk from here," Jim suggested.

We got out of the car and quickly realized that walking would be impossible. I still laugh when I think of the picture that we must have made as we crawled on hands and knees the rest of the way home.

On these long cold January nights I crave something that will warm and soothe me. I can think of nothing that is better able to do that than a steaming bowl of soup.

This recipe for Cream of Carrot Cheddar Cheese Soup has been a family favourite for years. Often I would make this soup when the girls were spending the day outdoors skiing or skating. Marg, Mary and Julia would come home chilled to the bone and ravenous from their exercise; this delicious soup would be their favourite "bone warmer." I find that I can almost make a meal of this soup. Any left over will make a nice beginning to a cold winter's evening meal.

Cream of Carrot Cheddar Cheese Soup

1 tbsp vegetable oil
1 onion, chopped
6 carrots, chopped
5 cups chicken stock
    (or chicken broth)
2 tbsp rice
1 tsp Worcestershire sauce
1/4 tsp dried thyme

1 tbsp parsley flakes
1 bay leaf
Dash of hot pepper sauce
Pinch of pepper (salt optional)
1 1/2 cups 2% milk
1 cup shredded old cheddar cheese

In a large saucepan, heat oil over medium heat; add onion and cook for 5 minutes (stirring occasionally). Add carrots, chicken stock, rice, Worcestershire sauce, thyme, parsley flakes, bay leaf, hot pepper sauce, pepper; bring to a boil. Reduce heat to low and simmer 25 minutes (or until carrots are tender). Discard bay leaf. In a blender purée the soup in batches; return to pan. Stir in milk. Bring to simmer; stir in cheddar cheese and cook over low heat until melted. Add salt to taste.

Serves 4

WE ARE A FAMILY of turkey lovers! The celebration of the new year offers yet another occasion for us to enjoy this delicious bird. We love it hot, cold, in sandwiches, soups and casseroles. We eat it for many meals before my son-in-law Bruce will declare himself "turkeyed out."

Two of our favourite recipes using leftover turkey are Turkey Squares and Turkey Pie.

Turkey Squares

3 cups finely diced leftover cooked turkey
2 cups fine soft breadcrumbs
1 cup turkey stock
2/3 cup finely diced celery
2 tbsp minced parsley
3 eggs, slightly beaten
1 tbsp lemon juice
2 tbsp finely diced onion
2/3 cups 10% cream
Salt and pepper to taste
Leftover turkey gravy

Mix together first 9 ingredients, add salt and pepper and place in a lightly buttered baking dish. Set the dish in a larger oven-proof dish and add water to a depth of 1/2 inch. Bake in a preheated oven at 350°F for 50–60 minutes. Cut into squares and serve with the turkey gravy (heated).

Serves 6–8

Turkey Pie

1/2 cup all-purpose flour
1 cup turkey stock, cold
3 cups turkey stock, hot
1 1/4 cups frozen green peas
2 cups stewed onions
2 cups chopped cooked carrots
2 cups diced leftover cooked turkey
Salt and pepper to taste
1 pkg ready-to-bake breadsticks
1 egg yolk

Combine flour and cold stock in a bowl. Place hot stock in a large heavy saucepan over medium heat, stir in flour mixture and cook, stirring constantly until it thickens. Add peas and cook several minutes more; stir in onions, carrots and turkey. Season to taste and pour into a large baking dish. Bake in a preheated 450°F oven 10–15 minutes. At the same time, weave breadsticks into a lattice the dimensions of the casserole. Place on a buttered cookie sheet, brush with egg yolk mixed with 1 tbsp water and bake along with the casserole 10 minutes more (20–25 minutes total for the casserole). When topping and casserole are done, press topping on to casserole and serve. (You can vary this recipe by adding celery or mushrooms as desired. Some people also prefer to use a traditional pastry covering, which would be baked on the casserole for the full 25 minutes or until nicely browned.)

Serves 6

EARLY SETTLERS IN CANADA came from many different social and economic backgrounds. They brought with them their own food habits, which had to be adapted to local conditions and native ingredients. One of the greatest influences on early Canadian cooking was that of the aboriginal people. Without their teaching, many of our early settlers would have perished. The natives knew how to use to best advantage the indigenous foods such as the plentiful fish and game. They grew patches of beans, pumpkin and corn and they knew how to preserve the corn by drying and powdering it.

One of the early traditional dishes of fish stew is most probably native and French in origin. We call it "chowder" but this word seems to have come from "chaudière," the large iron cooking pot used in the early days.

Growing up on Canada's east coast, I enjoyed many evenings of different fish chowders. Here is an easy but delicious chowder using scallops.

Scallop Chowder

2 onions, sliced

4 tbsp butter

2 cups scallops

2 cups boiling water

1 cup diced potatoes

4 cups scalded milk

Salt and pepper

Sauté onions in butter. Remove onions from pan. Cut up scallops and sauté in butter. Add onions, scallops and potatoes to boiling water. Simmer 30 minutes. Add scalded milk and simmer 15 minutes more. Add seasoning.

Serves 5

EVAN ESAR ONCE REMARKED of our climate, "Canada's climate is nine months of winter and three months late in the fall." There are times in January and February when I'm sure that we are in winter's eighth month. What better way is there to get rid of winter blues than to bake?

My great-grandchildren love these cookies, especially if they're served with a cup of hot chocolate.

Corn Flake Cookies

1 cup butter (room temperature)

1 cup white sugar

1 egg, lightly beaten

1 tsp vanilla

1 1/2 cups all-purpose flour

1 tsp cream of tartar

1/2 tsp salt

1 tsp baking soda

5 cups crushed corn flakes

Cream butter. Add sugar, egg, vanilla; mix well. Stir in flour, cream of tartar, salt, baking soda. Add corn flakes. Drop by spoonfuls 2 inches apart on an ungreased cookie sheet. Bake 10 minutes at 325°F.

MARION McMEEKAN, SECRETARY OF our local school and an excellent cook, passed along these next two recipes. She guarantees that they will warm even the coldest winter evenings.

Winter Pot Roast

1 pot roast (boneless cross cut beef or cut of your choice)
    3 lb approx
3 tbsp cooking oil
1 tsp salt (or less)
1/4 tsp pepper
1/2 cup grapefruit juice
1 can (7 1/2 oz) tomato sauce
3 medium onions, sliced
2 cloves garlic, finely diced
1 cup mushrooms (fresh or canned), sliced
2 tbsp brown sugar
1/2 tsp dry mustard
1/4 cup water
1/4 cup vinegar
1 tbsp Worcestershire sauce

In a Dutch oven or heavy pot, brown meat on all sides in the cooking oil. Drain off oil. Combine balance of ingredients and pour over roast. Cover and cook over low heat for 2–2 1/2 hours, turning roast on all sides (test with meat thermometer). Meat should be tender. Remove meat to warm platter to set for 10 minutes or so. Skim off any surface fat from sauce and dilute sauce with water or thicken with a little flour to suit your taste.

Variation: Combine ingredients from salt to garlic and pour over roast. Cover and cook over low heat 1 1/2 hours. Combine remaining ingredients and pour over roast. Cover and cook 1 hour more or until tender.

Broccoli and Cauliflower Casserole

2 cups broccoli florets

2 cups cauliflower florets

2 eggs

1/2 cup mayonnaise

1 medium onion, finely chopped

1 can cream of mushroom soup

1 cup sharp cheddar cheese, grated (reserve 1/2 cup)

1/2 cup melted butter

1 6-oz box croutons, crushed

Arrange broccoli and cauliflower in a greased 9 x 13-inch glass dish. Beat eggs; combine with mayonnaise, onion, soup and

1/2 cup cheese. Pour over the broccoli–cauliflower mixture. Spread remaining 1/2 cup of cheese over the casserole. Drizzle the melted butter over mixture. Spread crushed croutons on top. Bake 40 minutes at 325°F (350°F if using a non-glass pan).

Walk a mile in the winter twilight
Mark its whiteness and breathe its cold,
Reach your hands to the sunset embers,
Warm them there, and when you are old
There will be times when you recall it.

—*Grace Noll Crowell*

COMMUNITY BETTERMENT ALMOST ALWAYS takes money. Long ago women had little cash and their ways to raise it were few. So they turned to sewing, baking, knitting, crocheting and preserving in order to raise funds for such things as a library, new carpet for the church or a week at camp for needy children.

Often the "Church Supper" fundraisers offered the best of home-cooking in the area. These groups of dedicated women are still involved in projects in their communities and their coffee is enjoyed with homemade desserts all across the country.

Old-Time Ladies Auxiliary Coffee

1 cup regular grind coffee
1 egg, lightly beaten
1 egg shell, crushed
Few grains salt
8 cups cold water

Mix the coffee, beaten egg, crushed egg shell and salt. Wet with cold water and wring out a cloth bag large enough to permit the coffee to swell until double in bulk. Place the coffee inside the bag and tie shut. Bring the 8 cups of water to a full boil and pop in the bag of coffee. Let simmer 10 minutes, pushing the bag up and down several times. Remove the bag and serve the coffee at once.

Makes 12 excellent cups

MANY YEARS AGO MY husband George and I spent some weeks of January and February in England. You really need to have been there to understand just how cold and damp England can be at that time of year.

Much of our visit was spent in the beautiful Cotswold Hills area. Thankfully, almost every little town had a pub where the locals met to "hoist a pint" and dine on the "Ploughman's Lunch." I said "thankfully" because during all of our stay in England I believe the only time that I ever felt warm was sitting in front of the blazing fires that burned endlessly in these dining rooms. Occasionally, my teeth would stop chattering long enough to carry on a pleasant conversation with the interesting and friendly folk who were enjoying the soups and massive sandwiches that are the basics of the "Ploughman's Lunch" specials.

At one of the pubs near the village of Stanton, I was lucky enough to get the recipe for Stilton Cheese Soup. Stilton cheese, for those of you not familiar with the name, is a pungent but delicious cheese not unlike a Danish blue cheese but with a sharper flavour. Here, then, is the recipe for Stilton Cheese Soup guaranteed to ward off even the damp cold of an English winter.

Stilton Cheese Soup

1/4 cup butter

1 onion, skinned and finely chopped

2 celery sticks, cleaned and sliced

6 tbsp flour

3 1/2–4 tbsp dry white wine

3 3/4 cups chicken stock

1 1/4 cups milk

3/4 cup Stilton cheese, crumbled

1/2 cup plus 2 tbsp English cheddar cheese, grated

Salt and freshly ground pepper

5 tbsp fresh heavy whipping cream

Melt the butter in a saucepan, add the vegetables and fry gently for 5 minutes. Stir in the flour and cook for 1 minute. Remove from the heat, stir in the wine and stock, return to the heat, bring to a boil and simmer for 30 minutes. Add the milk and cheeses, stirring constantly; season. Stir in the fresh cream. Rub through a strainer or sieve, or purée in a blender and reheat without boiling. Garnish with croutons if desired.

Serves 4–6

SATURDAY NIGHTS IN OUR home were usually spent in eager anticipation of the now-immortal words of Foster Hewitt, "He shoots! He scores!" To say that we were hockey fans would be an understatement. We were hockey nuts! Before the days of television, we would gather round the radio to listen to Foster Hewitt's wonderful descriptions of the happenings on the ice. How easy it was to close our eyes and "see" the "Rocket" swoop in on goal. "Richard shoots! Oh, what a save by Broda!"

Saturday night dinners were also eagerly awaited. George would make a huge pot of spaghetti sauce and meatballs early in the day and the delicious smell would permeate every corner of our house. George got his meatball recipe from Win Gosse, a longtime friend whose Italian background shows in the recipe given below.

For me Saturday night is still "spaghetti night" and Win's meatballs are just as delicious as ever.

Spaghetti Sauce

1 28-oz tin tomatoes
1 12-oz tin tomato paste
1/2 cup chopped green pepper
3 cloves garlic
4 tbsp Italian seasoning
1 tsp each salt and pepper
1/4 tsp sugar
2 cups water

Place all ingredients (except water) in a blender. (Thanks to this time-saving device, which saves us from chopping and mashing.) Blend until smooth. Transfer to a large saucepan and add water.

Meatballs

1 lb ground beef
3/4 lb ground pork or veal
1/2 cup finely chopped green pepper
1 egg
1/2 cup breadcrumbs
1 tsp each salt and pepper

Combine all ingredients and form into 2-inch balls. Brown meatballs in 2 tbsp oil in a frypan or place meatballs on a flat oven pan and brown at 350°F (about 10 minutes). Add meatballs to the Spaghetti Sauce. Cover and allow the sauce to simmer at least 2 hours. (We often simmer 6–7 hours.) If thicker sauce is desired, remove lid for approximately 1 hour to allow the sauce to thicken.

Another winter favourite of ours, which we might have as a late-night dessert after our spaghetti dinner, is the Hot Milk Cake made from a recipe that was given to me by my dear friend Kay Kennedy. It is her mother's recipe.

Hot Milk Cake

Mix together:

1 cup sugar

2 eggs

Sift in:

1 cup flour

1 1/2 tsp baking powder

1/2 tsp salt

Add 1 tbsp butter melted in 1/2 cup warm milk to above ingredients. Bake in an 8-inch square pan in a 350°F oven for 25 minutes.

Topping: Mix together 2 tbsp butter, 1/2 cup shredded coconut, 1/2 cup walnuts (chopped), 5 tbsp brown sugar, 2 tbsp milk. Spread over hot cake and broil for a few minutes.

Tobogganing and skiing—two favourite winter activities.

February

lthough February often brings us much harsh winter weather, this month also gives us a lovely day of celebration. St. Valentine's Day honours Saint Valentine, a Christian martyr who died in the third century. The celebration associated with Saint Valentine probably derived from the ancient Roman feast of Lupercalia, which was held on February 15. On that day it was the custom for young Roman men and maidens to draw partners for the coming year. As the number of Christians increased in the Empire, Lupercalia became linked to the feast of St. Valentine held on February 14. And so, Saint Valentine became known as the patron saint of lovers.

My late husband George was an incurable romantic. No matter how tight our budget was (in a minister's family the budget was *always* tight), George would plan something very special for Valentine's Day. My happiest memory is of our last Valentine's Day together. George sent me off to a ladies auxiliary meeting and during my absence he put together a wonderful meal complete with a beautifully set table including candles and fresh-cut flowers. After dinner he turned on some soft music and we danced together as we had done so often in our younger years. I treasure the memory of that evening.

With George's encouragement our family has always celebrated Valentine's Day with great enthusiasm. Often we spend days planning the special meal that usually includes an appetizer, soup or salad, entrée and an especially alluring dessert (chocolate is our usual choice). As our family has grown we have found it expedient to make this a combined effort, with each smaller family group responsible for some part of the dinner that we will enjoy together.

Here, then, are our favourite recipes combined to create the "St. Valentine's Day Dinner Delight."

Hot Crabmeat Appetizer

1 8-oz pkg cream cheese

1 1/2 cups (7 1/2-oz can) drained flaked crabmeat

2 tbsp finely chopped onion

2 tbsp milk

1/2 tsp cream-style horseradish

1/4 tsp salt (optional)

Dash pepper

1/3 cup sliced almonds, toasted

Combine softened cream cheese, crabmeat, onion, milk, horseradish and seasonings. Mix until well blended. Spoon into 9-inch pie plate (or oven-proof dish); sprinkle on toasted almonds. Bake in a preheated 375°F oven for 15 minutes. Serve with a variety of crackers or melba rounds.

Romaine and Watercress Salad

1 head romaine lettuce, washed and broken into bite-size
*   pieces*
1 cup chopped watercress
8–10 radishes, sliced
2–3 green onions, chopped

Mix all ingredients in salad bowl.

Dressing:
5 tbsp olive oil
2 tbsp wine vinegar
1 clove garlic
1/8 tsp freshly ground pepper
1/4 tsp tarragon

Mix in a small jar or cruet. Pour over salad and toss until leaves are lightly covered.

Chicken Divan

4 boneless chicken breasts
1 10-oz pkg frozen broccoli
1 can cream of chicken soup
1/3 cup mayonnaise

2 tbsp lemon juice

1/2 tsp curry powder

1 cup shredded sharp cheddar cheese

1/2 cup bread crumbs

2 tbsp melted butter or margarine

Precook chicken breasts in a covered baking dish at 325°F for 40 minutes. Remove chicken and cut in pieces. Place chicken pieces and broccoli in a lightly greased casserole. Combine soup, mayonnaise, lemon juice, curry powder and cheese. Pour over chicken and broccoli. Sprinkle bread crumbs on top. Pour melted butter or margarine over casserole. Bake in a preheated 350°F oven for 45 minutes to 1 hour.

Serves 4

I like to serve Chicken Divan with egg noodles that have been buttered and had chopped parsley added.

Honey-Glazed Carrots

Wash and scrape 8 carrots. Slice thinly lengthwise. Boil in small quantity of water to desired tenderness. Drain. Add 4 tbsp butter and 1/4 cup honey to pan. Simmer until carrots are glazed.

Serves 4

Black Bottom Pie

1 1/2 cups crushed gingersnaps
1/2 cup butter, melted
1 envelope unflavoured gelatin
1 cup sugar
1 tbsp cornstarch
4 eggs, separated
2 cups milk
2 squares unsweetened chocolate, melted
1 tsp vanilla
2 tbsp rum
1/8 tsp cream of tartar

Blend crushed gingersnaps and butter in a small saucepan. Press evenly over bottom and side of a 9-inch pie plate. Bake in a preheated 300°F oven for 5 minutes; cool; chill.

Combine gelatin, 1/2 cup of the sugar, cornstarch and egg yolks in a large saucepan; beat until blended. Stir in milk until smooth. Cook over low heat, stirring constantly, until custard thickens. Blend 1 cup of the custard with the chocolate and vanilla; pour into crust; chill. Stir rum into remaining custard; chill until it begins to thicken. Beat egg whites with cream of tartar until foamy. Beat in remaining 1/2 cup sugar gradually until meringue forms soft peaks. Fold into thickened custard. Spoon over chocolate layer. Chill 2 hours or until firm.

Garnish with whipped cream and chocolate curls, if you wish.

May the skies above be cloudless
On this February day,
May the sun beam warm and golden
As it shines along your way.

—A.K. Roberts

IN FEBRUARY MOST FISHERMEN will have stored their tackle away until spring. Not so the hardiest of all fishermen—the ice fisherman. He gets out his spud, skimmer, bucket and tilts and heads for the bitterly cold, windswept pond or lake. These ardent anglers insist that ice fishing is the most satisfying way to spend a winter's day. For the life of me I can't understand the mind that thinks it pleasurable to sit for hours in frigid weather wiggling a string in the oft-vain hope that something will bite.

According to my friend Jake, perch, pike and pickerel are the best of the winter fish. Their firm texture is a result of the cold water. Jake is one of this strange breed who will head out ice fishing weekend after weekend and seem to enjoy it immensely. This is his recipe for Fried Pickerel.

Fried Pickerel

Clean, wash and dry the fish. Roll the fish in salt-and-peppered flour, or dip in egg and roll in seasoned cracker crumbs. Use enough oil in a heavy frypan that the fish can float. Bring the oil to a boil slowly and then fry the fish quickly until golden brown and crisp on the outside.

Fortunately, it isn't necessary to be an ice fisherman to have a fish dinner in winter. Thanks to the wonder of frozen foods, it is possible to enjoy fish of many varieties all year round. Here are two more ways to prepare the "catch of the day."

Baked Fish with Sour Cream

Split and remove bones from fish. Rub inside and out with butter and paprika. Broil until lightly browned. Cover with sour cream. Cover the pan and bake in 325°F oven for about 40 minutes.

Baked Fish with Almond Sauce

Roll fish fillets in seasoned bread crumbs. Let stand for 1/2 hour to dry. Brown the fish in melted butter, then bake in 325°F oven for about 40 minutes. Sauté 1/2 cup blanched almonds in 6 tbsp of butter. Season to taste.

Baked Fish with Almond Sauce may be garnished with parsley and served with rice.

WHEN I WAS A young bride, George and I moved to a parish in a farming community. To greet the new parishioners, we gave a small reception in the church basement (known as the meeting room). Hoping to make a good impression, I made dozens of "tea" sandwiches—small triangles or squares of bread with egg salad decorated with an olive "flower", or ham salad on tiny strips of bread rolled around a pickle. At the time these were considered to be the last word in elegance in the gracious homes of east coast cities. I was so proud of my trays of little sandwiches until I heard one of the farmers talking to his wife. "Sakes alive, Martha, maybe we'd best have a meeting about the new minister's salary. Will you look at the size of the sandwiches his poor young wife has made!" I learned pretty quickly that large quantities of good food were what was expected by these hardworking men of the community. Elegance was unnecessary!

Early in our married life, I was given the responsibility of providing the "goodies" at George's church meetings. Fortunately, the ladies of the parish were more than anxious to share their recipes with the minister's wife and I was soon able to whip up something quite edible at a moment's notice. Now my friends and I get together to enjoy one of these recipes nearly every week and they are as delicious as I remember them from those years so long ago.

Fresh Apple Coffee Cake

1 cup flour
1/2 tsp salt
1 tsp baking soda

2 cups cored, peeled and diced apples (any apples may be
    used)
1 egg
1/4 cup salad oil
1 cup sugar
1 tsp ground cinnamon
1/4 tsp nutmeg
1/2 cup chopped walnuts

Sift flour, salt and baking soda. Set aside. Place apples in a
medium-size bowl. Break egg over the apples; add oil, sugar,
cinnamon, nutmeg and nuts. Blend thoroughly. Stir dry mixture into the apple mixture just until flour is moist. (Mixture
will appear rather dry.) Spread in a greased 8-inch square
pan. Bake in a preheated 350°F oven for 40–45 minutes. Let
stand for 10 minutes, then turn out on a wire rack.

   For a decorative touch, place a paper doily over the cake
and dust with powdered sugar.

WINTER HAS A VERY special beauty and its own particular joys. Snow-covered hillsides are bright with painted
sleds and the sound of children's laughter. Skiers seem to
have wings as they fly down the high slopes. Every frozen
pond is a figure skater's paradise or a hockey player's arena.

   My great-grandchildren, Justin and Jenny, spend as
much time as possible skating on our local pond. After an

afternoon of hockey with their friends, they love to come in and snack on Oatmeal Muffins and hot chocolate. This recipe is one of their favourites.

Oatmeal Muffins

1 cup buttermilk
1 cup quick-cooking oatmeal
1/2 cup light brown sugar
1 cup sifted flour
1/2 tsp salt
1/2 tsp baking soda
2 tsp baking powder
1 egg, beaten
1/4 cup melted shortening

Combine buttermilk, oatmeal and brown sugar, and let stand 10 minutes. Sift flour and salt, baking soda and baking powder. Add beaten egg to oatmeal mixture, then add melted shortening, mixing well. Now stir in the flour mixture, using only enough strokes to moisten all ingredients; don't beat. Fill 12 greased muffin cups (or paper-lined cups). Bake in a preheated 375°F oven for 20–25 minutes.

Life itself can't give you joy,
Unless you really will it;
Life just gives you time and space
It's up to you to fill it.

—*Anonymous*

ON THESE SNOWY FEBRUARY days as the snow-ploughs struggle to clear the roads, I like to remember many years ago when we lived on Canada's east coast. Teams of eight or ten horses dragged a huge roller over snowy roads to make them suitable for sleighing—a simple, suitable means of winter transportation. Coming in after a horse-drawn sleigh ride, we would be ready for a wonderful hot meal. Often mother would have left a stew cooking so that dinner would be ready when we returned. One of my favourite stews is a Lamb Stew. This recipe is a special treat provided by the family of my son-in-law Bruce.

Lamb Stew

2 1/2 lb lamb stew meat
2 tbsp butter
Sprinkle of sugar
Salt and pepper (to taste)
3 tsp flour
2 1/2 cups lamb stock or water
1 bay leaf

1 clove garlic, minced

1 onion, chopped

1 stalk celery, diced

2 carrots, diced

1 cup tomatoes

3 cups mixed vegetables (potatoes, peas)

Brown lamb pieces in butter. Sprinkle with sugar. Stir in salt, pepper and flour. Reduce heat and cook 10 minutes. Stir in stock or water and bring to the boiling point. Reduce heat to simmer. Add bay leaf, garlic, onion, celery, carrots and tomatoes. Cover tightly and simmer for 1 1/2 hours. Sauté mixed vegetables, then add to lamb mixture. Continue cooking until lamb and vegetables are tender.

Serves 6

Edna's Aromatic Bath

This recipe for an aromatic bath came from an old cookbook belonging to my mother. Boil the following herbs in a bag for thirty minutes in six quarts of water: lavender, mint, thyme, sage, rosemary, marjoram, wormwood and fennel. Add this water to bath water. Do not remain more than thirty minutes in this bath.

OFTEN THE MONTH OF February marks the beginning of Lent and its forty days to Easter. With the fasting and cleansing of the spirit during this holy time went many curious customs in ancient times. For instance, the day before

Shrove Tuesday was known as Collop Monday. Slices of bacon or ham, taken from carcasses hung up for the winter, were known as "collops" and feasts used large portions of these meats in order to get rid of the meat that the fasts of Lent would leave to rot. The ancient Greek church gave us the custom of eating pancakes on Mardi Gras (Shrove Tuesday). On this day before Ash Wednesday—the beginning of Lent—milk, eggs, cheese and pancakes were the fare for the day.

The word "Lent" in the Saxon language meant "spring." Originally Lent began on a Sunday and ended on Easter Eve. That made forty-two days and if you subtracted the six Sundays (it was unlawful to fast on Sundays in olden times) that left thirty-six days. Pope Gregory added to Lent the four days of the week before that Sunday, and that day which we now call Ash Wednesday thereby became the first day of Lent. The date of Ash Wednesday is determined each year by the full moon nearest to the spring equinox (usually March 21st).

Coming up to the season of Lent it seems that we are given a special treat to make up for the sacrifices to be made. Served right from the oven the Hot Cross Bun is a delicious breakfast treat.

Hot Cross Buns

1 cup milk, scalded
1/2 cup sugar
3 tbsp melted butter
1/2 tsp salt

1 yeast cake
1/4 cup warm water
1 egg, well beaten
3 cups flour
1/2 tsp cinnamon
1/2 cup currants
1 tsp grated lemon peel
1 pinch ground cloves
1 egg, well beaten
Confectioners' sugar and milk

Combine scalded milk, sugar, butter, salt. When lukewarm, add yeast cake dissolved in the 1/4 cup water. Then add egg and mix well. Sift flour and cinnamon together, and stir into yeast mixture. Add currants, lemon peel and cloves. Mix thoroughly. Cover and let rise in a warm place until double in size. Shape dough into round buns and place on a well-buttered baking sheet. Let rise again. Brush top of each bun with egg. Make a cross on each bun with a sharp knife. Bake in a hot oven (400°F) for 20 minutes. Remove from oven and brush the crosses with confectioners' sugar moistened with milk.

Have you noticed that
as we get older,
the days get longer
but the years get shorter?

Taking little sister for a ride in the wagon.

March

In March, before spring is really apparent, the sap in the roots of the maple trees begins its upward journey in the trunks towards the branches. Long before the white man came to North America, the aboriginal people collected the sap from the sugar maple trees. To boil the sap and thicken it they tossed stones, heated white-hot, into watertight baskets. Today, many farmers tap the trees on their properties to make maple syrup and provide themselves with an off-season income. Those who invite visitors to join in the "sugaring off" use the original sap-gathering methods: the baskets hung on the trees, the gathering of the run, the fires burning in the sap house and the boiling down of the sap to make the thick delicious pure maple syrup or candy.

Some years ago George and I were visiting with friends in Québec City, just about this time of year. They suggested a trip to a sugarbush, so the four of us travelled south from Québec City to the small town of Beauceville. It was a glorious bright day and we joined about twenty others in collecting the sap buckets and stoking the fire in the sap house to boil down the syrup. At noon we all sat at large tables in an adjoining log cabin and enjoyed maple-cured ham slices and hot, syrup-covered pancakes. I can remember to this day the beauty of the snowy woods and the pleasure of partaking in this very Canadian activity.

There are so many ways to use pure maple syrup and although there are maple syrup substitutes on the market these days, none can match the delicious flavour of the real thing.

Maple Baked Ham is one of my favourite ways of using maple syrup.

Maple Baked Ham

1 ham

1 cup maple syrup per 5 lb of ham

3–4 tbsp all-purpose flour

To bake the ham, remove the skin. Place ham in a shallow roasting pan. Bake in a 325°F oven about 20 minutes per lb. When about half done, remove drippings and set aside. Pour the maple syrup over the ham; baste every 20 minutes until done. Remove from oven. Pour off maple-flavoured drippings into a saucepan. Add the drippings previously set aside and heat. Thicken with the flour; serve as a sauce.

Buckwheat Cakes are just a little different from the ordinary pancake. Buckwheat flour adds a taste that is not your "run-of-the-mill" pancake flavour.

Buckwheat Cakes and Maple Syrup

1 yeast cake

1/4 cup warm water

1 tsp sugar

4 cups buckwheat flour
2 cups water
1 tsp salt

Dissolve yeast cake in warm water. Add sugar. Make a stiff batter of flour, water, salt. Add yeast. Let rise. Let batter stand overnight in a warm place, to be used for breakfast. Spoon onto hot griddle. Brown both sides. Serve hot with maple syrup.

Serves 4

Maple Mousse is a delicious light dessert. Many people enjoy chocolate mousse—Maple Mousse is for maple syrup lovers.

Maple Mousse

2 eggs, separated
1/8 tsp salt
1 cup maple syrup
1 cup whipped cream
1 tsp vanilla

Beat egg yolks. Add salt and maple syrup. Cook in top of double boiler until mixture thickens. Cool. Fold in stiffly beaten egg whites, then cream. Add vanilla. Freeze in serving dishes.

Serves 6

SOME YEARS AGO MY husband George and I were travelling through the scenic Berkshire hills in western
Massachusetts. In the small township of Hancock we came
across a tiny village made up of eighteen buildings on about
one thousand acres of beautiful farm and woodland. It was the
Hancock Shaker Village and we spent several hours in the
historical museum learning much about Shakers and their
contribution to the culture of America. Below is just a little
of what we learned and a couple of recipes of typical Shaker
cooking.

In 1758 Ann Lees, a twenty-two-year-old unschooled tex-
tile worker and cook, joined the Wardley Society, a group of
dissenters led by Quaker tailors living in Bolton-on-the-Moors,
a town about twelve miles from Manchester, England. These
religious enthusiasts were inspired by a radical group of
Calvinists known as the "French Prophets." The "mighty
shakes" induced by their spiritual gyrations led to their being
called "Shaking Quakers" or "Shakers." After seeing a vision
of Christ, Ann Lees took the title "Mother of the New
Creation." Mother Ann and eight followers emigrated to New
York and, in the wilderness up the Hudson River, near what
is now Albany, established the first Shaker settlement in the
New World. Over the years the Shaker communities were
established throughout New England and in Ohio, Indiana
and Kentucky.

In 1882 Mary Whitcher (or Sister Mary) wrote: "The
Shakers recognize the fact that good food properly cooked
and well digested is the basis of good health." The Shaker
principle was, "Eat hearty and decent, and clear out your
plate."

"Shaker Your Plate" is a typical admonition from a people to whom waste was an affront to God. In *Our Shaker Home, 1830,* these verses explain:

> *We're willing to state—*
> *Eat hearty and decent,*
> *And clear out your plate—*
> *Be thankful to heaven—*
> *For what we receive,*
> *And not make a mixture*
> *Or compound to leave*

> *We find of those bounties*
> *Which heaven doth give,*
> *That some live to eat,*
> *And, that some eat to live—*
> *That some think of nothing*
> *But pleasing the taste,*
> *And care very little*
> *How much they do waste.*

Shaker culinary habits included the use of unusual spices and savoury herbs. The result was cuisine that was sophisticated for nineteenth-century America and important in the development of modern American cooking.

Shaker Herb Soup

Sister Amelia's Shaker Recipes

1 tbsp butter

2 tbsp chopped chives

2 tbsp minced chervil

2 tbsp minced sorrel

1/2 tsp finely cut tarragon

1 cup finely chopped celery

4 cups chicken broth

Salt and pepper to taste

Sprinkle sugar

6 slices white toast

Dash nutmeg

Grated cheddar cheese

Melt butter in skillet, then add herbs and celery and simmer for 3 minutes. Add broth and seasonings. Cook gently for 20 minutes. Place slices of toast in tureen and pour soup over them. Add nutmeg and sprinkle with grated cheese. Serve very hot.

Makes 4–6 servings

Shaker Herb Bread

Hancock Shaker Village, Massachusetts

2 cups milk

1/4 cup sugar

1/4 tsp salt

2 envelopes active dry yeast

2 eggs, well beaten

1 tsp powdered nutmeg or cloves

2 tsp crumbled dried sage leaves

4 tsp caraway seeds

1 tsp dried rosemary

1 tsp dried dill

7 1/2–8 cups presifted flour

1/4 cup melted butter

Scald milk. Stir in sugar and salt, cool to lukewarm. Add yeast. Stir well until completely dissolved. Add eggs, nutmeg, herbs and 4 cups of flour. Beat until smooth. Add butter and enough of the remaining flour to make a soft dough that is easy to handle. Turn onto lightly floured board. Knead until smooth and elastic. Place dough in a greased bowl—cover—let rise about 2 hours or until doubled in bulk. Grease 2 loaf pans. Punch dough down. Divide in half. Fill each pan—cover—let rise again 1 hour or until doubled in bulk. Preheat oven to 425°F. Bake for 15 minutes. Reduce heat to 375°F. Bake 35 minutes. (A nice addition is 2 tsp celery seeds.)

Yields 2 loaves

O Ireland isn't it grand you look—
Like a bride in her rich adornin'
And with all the pent-up love of my heart
I bid you top o' the mornin'.

—*John Locke*

MY FATHER WAS OF Irish background and he revelled in the celebration of their special day. He would be proudly "wearin' the green" and wishing to all a "Happy St. Patrick's Day." Over the years I have found that two qualities make the Irish very special. The one is their profound sense of loyalty to their homeland and friends; the other is the strength of their family ties.

Celebration of St. Patrick's Day in our home always meant serving "green' food—food that was naturally green or something that we could make green with food colouring. Key Lime Pie is a delicious way to fill the bill.

Key Lime Pie

4 eggs, separated
3 tbsp sugar
1/2 cup plus 1/2 cup white corn syrup
1/3 cup lime juice
1 tbsp grated lime rind
1/4 tsp salt

1 envelope unflavoured gelatin
1/4 cup cold water
1 9-inch pie shell, baked and chilled

Beat egg yolks until fluffy, then beat in the sugar and 1/2 cup of the corn syrup. Add the lime juice, grated lime rind and salt and cook over low heat, stirring constantly until smooth and slightly thickened. Remove from heat. Soften the gelatin in the cold water and add to the lime mixture, stirring until dissolved; then cool. Beat the egg whites until stiff, and then beat in remaining corn syrup very gradually with a rotary beater. Fold into the lime mixture and fill the pie shell; chill until firm. (If desired, a few drops of green food colouring may be added to the filling—for a real St. Patrick's green.)

Serves 8

*May you be in Heaven an hour before
the Devil knows you're gone.*

—Irish proverb

THE "SPRING FEVER" PHENOMENON catches me unawares every year. One day I am sitting in a chair reading a book—in my winter mode; the next I am overcome by the desire to clean windows, tidy cupboards, rake out the garden or take a long walk in the slightly warmer sunshine.

Thankfully this fever also strikes my daughter Marg at just about the same time and we are able to begin our cleaning chores together. As they say, "Many hands make light work."

Marg and I also like to make up some "do ahead" meals, something that will allow us to spend our days preparing our gardens or cleaning cupboards without having to use much of our afternoon in preparation of the evening meal. Noodle Pie can be made up and baked, then reheated or served cold for supper.

Noodle Pie

Unbaked pastry for a 2-crust pie

1/2 cup milk

2 cups cooked flat noodles

1 cup minced baked or boiled ham

1 tbsp butter, cut into slivers

3 tbsp sour cream

3 tbsp minced onion

Freshly ground black pepper

Line a 9-inch pie pan with pastry. Refrigerate until well chilled. Chill pastry for the top crust. Heat milk (do not allow to boil) and pour over noodles in large bowl. Let noodles soak for 2 or 3 minutes, then place in a colander and drain off the milk. Line the chilled pastry in the pie pan with 1/3 of the drained noodles. Cover with 1/3 of the ham. Dot with 1 tsp of the butter slivers. Add 1 tbsp sour cream, 1 tbsp minced onion and a generous sprinkling of pepper. Repeat the layers twice. Cover with pastry dough and seal the edges. Prick the surface several times with a fork. Place in a pre-heated 400°F oven and bake 10 minutes; reduce heat to 325°F and bake for 20–25 minutes or until the crust is a light golden brown. May be served hot or cold.

Serves 8 as an appetizer, 4 as an entrée

THE FIRST DAY OF spring is also the birthday of my great-granddaughter Bethany. Since chocolate is the flavour of choice for birthday cakes in our family, I have quite a large collection of chocolate cake recipes. This is my favourite.

Chocolate Cake

1 cup unsweetened cocoa powder

2 cups boiling water

2 3/4 cup unsifted all-purpose flour

1/2 tsp baking powder

1/2 tsp salt

1 cup butter, softened

2 1/2 cups granulated sugar

4 large eggs

1 1/2 tsp vanilla extract

Filling:

4 bars (8 oz each) white baking chocolate, chopped

2 cups heavy cream

Frosting:

1 12-oz pkg semisweet chocolate pieces

1/2 cup half and half cream

1 cup butter

1 box (1 lb) confectioners' sugar

Preheat oven to 350°F. Grease and flour 3 9-inch round cake pans; set aside. Place cocoa in a medium bowl; gradually stir in 2 cups boiling water, stirring until blended. Set aside to cool completely. On a sheet of waxed paper, combine flour, baking powder and 1/2 tsp salt; set aside. In a large bowl beat 1 cup butter with granulated sugar with an electric mixer on high speed until mixture is light and fluffy. Add eggs, 1 at a time, beating well after each addition. Beat in vanilla. Alternately add 1/4 of flour mixture and 1/3 cocoa mixture; place in prepared pans—dividing evenly. Bake 25 minutes. Cool in pans 10 minutes. Remove and cool on wire racks.

Filling: In the top of double boiler placed over hot—not boiling—water, combine white chocolate and 1/4 cup heavy cream. Heat, stirring, until white chocolate melts and mixture is smooth. Remove from heat; pour into large bowl. Stir in remaining heavy cream; refrigerate until very cold. With mixer at high speed, beat filling ingredients together until stiff. Reserve 1 1/4 cups of the mixture; place remainder between cooled cake layers, dividing evenly.

Frosting: In a medium saucepan, over medium heat, combine chocolate pieces, half and half cream and 1 cup butter. Cook, stirring, until mixture is smooth. Transfer mixture to large mixing bowl; with electric mixer on high speed, beat in confectioners' sugar. Place bowl in larger bowl of ice and water; at high speed beat until frosting is firm enough to spread. With a metal spatula cover the top and sides of the cake with frosting.

To decorate the cake: Place the 1 1/4 cups reserved filling in a pastry bag fitted with a star tip. Pipe mixture into 8 rosettes, spacing evenly around the top edge of the cake. Refrigerate until ready to serve.

Serves 12

Caution: This cake is highly addictive—eating large pieces has been known to add inches to waistlines and hips.

Three sisters in their Sunday best.

April

The vernal equinox has come and gone and these warm days of April have given many of us our first chance to spend some time outdoors. The birds are back! Robins are busy digging for worms in the new shoots of grass that are forcing their way up through the old brown cover. Crocuses and daffodils are coming into bloom.

Spring is especially welcome in the northern climes. After what seems to be endless snow and cold weather, we delight in being outside. A walk through the neighbourhood can be a wonderful way to welcome the new season. My friend Lila and I try to do this early in the spring and we take our time—pausing to look at the new shoots of grass coming up, checking to see if we can see the beginning leaf buds, or just enjoying the warm sunshine that we have missed for so long. I like these words of Martin Luther: "Our Lord has written the promise of the Resurrection, not in books alone, but in every leaf in springtime."

In the Christian religion Easter marks the time of renewal, of new beginnings. Good Friday, the day of Jesus' crucifixion, always had special meaning for George and me. The number of services during Holy Week greatly increased his responsibilities and by Friday he was very tired. Yet the solemnity of the day seemed to give him renewed strength. How I loved to hear him, at the closing of the afternoon services, when he sang, unaccompanied, the Reproaches. The joy of the Resurrection on Easter Sunday made these services some of the happiest and most beautiful of the year.

Very often families get together after church and enjoy a special Easter dinner. In our home ham and scalloped potatoes were a popular choice for this meal that marked the end of the Lenten season. This tradition remains with us today and I offer our family's recipes for Baked Virginia Ham with Madeira Gravy and Scalloped Potatoes.

Baked Virginia Ham with Madeira Gravy

1 cured Virginia ham, bone in

50–60 cloves

1 cup Madeira wine

Trim the rind away from the ham leaving an exposed layer of fat. With a small sharp knife, score the exposed fat in a diamond pattern cutting almost through to where the meat begins. Insert 1 clove at each intersection of 2 knife scores all over the fat side. Bake the ham in a 325°F oven about 30 minutes per lb basting occasionally with the drippings. When ready, transfer the ham to a meat platter. Pour the Madeira into the baking pan. Over medium heat on the stovetop, scrape the drippings and combine with the Madeira to make gravy. Cook until heated through. Skim off about half the liquid fat and pour what is left into the gravy boat to accompany the ham.

Scalloped Potatoes

6–8 potatoes, peeled and thinly sliced
2–3 onions, peeled, sliced and separated into rings
Flour
Butter
Salt and pepper
Milk

In a greased 9 x 13-inch casserole dish arrange a layer (2–3 slices deep) of sliced potatoes. Arrange onion rings on top of potato slices. Sprinkle enough flour to lightly cover the layer. Dot with butter and sprinkle with salt and pepper. Continue layering. Pour milk into the casserole to the level of the top of the onions on the top layer of the casserole. Cook in a 350°F oven approximately 30–45 minutes. Casserole is ready when potatoes and onions are easily penetrated with a fork. Top will become brown.

Serves 6–8

SPRING AND EARLY SUMMER also bring fiddlehead greens. Fiddleheads are the unopened fronds of fiddlehead ferns, which can be cooked and served as a vegetable or used in salads. Fiddleheads with Lemon Butter would make a nice accompaniment to a special Easter dinner.

Fiddleheads with Lemon Butter

1 lb fiddleheads
2 tbsp melted butter
Juice of 1 lemon
Salt and pepper to taste

Wash the fiddleheads carefully so as not to break them. Place washed fiddleheads in boiling water. Boil 5–6 minutes or until tender. Drain. Place in serving dish. On the stovetop (or in a microwave oven) melt butter. Squeeze the juice of 1 lemon into the melted butter. Pour lemon butter over the fiddleheads and toss them lightly until they are covered. Add salt and pepper to taste. Serve immediately.

Fiddleheads are an excellent addition to a salad. To use: wash fiddleheads, then place in boiling, lightly salted water. Cook until tender. Drain. Refrigerate until chilled. They add a flavour of broccoli and asparagus and are a delicious and different way to enhance a chef's salad or a jellied vegetable salad.

O! How this spring of love resembleth
The uncertain glory of an April day!

—William Shakespeare

MANY YEARS AGO THE reception welcoming the new minister to town was known as the "Donation Party." The parishioners would bring bags of potatoes, large squares of salt pork, pounds of butter and whatever they had in abundance in their homes. In the days of little refrigeration, it was almost impossible to keep such large quantities of food unspoiled until eaten. Very often the minister would take a portion of the donated goods to another town where he would exchange the food for things that his family needed more. If you asked anyone why the people didn't present the minister with cash, the most welcome gift of all, the reply would always be the same. "Folks wouldn't do it. This is the way it has always been done."

In a minister's family it seemed that money was often in short supply. This recipe for Old-Fashioned Scrap Soup was given to me by my mother. Many's the time this delicious soup provided a meal when, at the end of the salary, there was more month left.

Old-Fashioned Scrap Soup

2 cups scraps

5 cups water

Salt and pepper to taste

(Bouillon cubes are a modern but good-tasting addition)

Scraps may be the combination of a few lettuce leaves, celery tops, a bit of meat or fish or leftover vegetables. I often make use of a chop bone, end of raw onion or any leftover that doesn't seem to have an immediate use. Scraps should be stored in the refrigerator until there are enough to make soup.

Simmer the scraps and water for about 1 1/2 hours. If you have no meat or bones to use, 2 or 3 bouillon cubes will add flavour to the soup. Remove bones from the soup. Years ago, we put the soup through a sieve—today it can be whirled in a blender—before seasoning to taste with salt and pepper. Serve piping hot.

Makes 6 servings

Butter Corn Sticks are a tasty treat to enjoy with Scrap Soup.

Butter Corn Sticks

1/3 cup butter or margarine

2 1/4 cups sifted flour

4 tsp baking powder

2 tbsp sugar

1 tsp salt

1/4 cup milk

1 cup cream-style canned corn

Melt the butter in a 9 x 13-inch baking pan. Sift the flour with the baking powder, sugar and salt. Stir in milk and corn. Mix, then turn out onto a floured surface. Knead lightly, then roll to about 1/2 inch in thickness. Cut into 1-inch strips. Lay each strip in the melted butter, turning to coat each side. Bake in a 450°F oven for about 18 minutes or until crispy brown. Serve at once.

Another inexpensive but very satisfying meal is Baked Bean and Apple Casserole. The apples make a nice variation for an old standard dish.

Baked Bean and Apple Casserole

2 cups dried navy beans

2/3 tsp salt

2 medium apples, peeled, cored and sliced

1/2 cup light brown sugar

1/4 lb fat salt pork, sliced

Soak beans overnight in water, covering well. In the morning, drain and just barely cover in fresh water. Add salt, cover and simmer about 1 hour, or until beans are just tender. Drain, reserving liquid. In a bean pot or heavy casserole make alternate layers of the beans and the sliced apples, ending in a bean layer. Sprinkle each layer with a part of the brown sugar. Lay the salt pork slices (sliced fat bacon is an acceptable alternative) on top of the beans. Pour in the reserved bean liquid just to the level of the top of the beans. Cover and bake in a 350°F oven for about 2 hours; the longer they bake, the better they'll be. If the beans appear dry during baking, add a little more of the reserved liquid so the beans are moist when done.

OFTEN IN APRIL, MARG, Bruce and I like to host a "Spring Brunch." We invite our neighbours and friends to come on a Sunday after church and we enjoy a buffet-style brunch. It gives us a chance to renew friendships that are often put on hold during the winter months when we rarely see one another.

The next several recipes are just a few of the dishes that have been a part of these brunches.

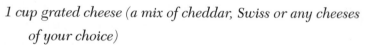

Quiche Lorraine

1 large pie shell

3 eggs

3/4 cup whipping cream

3/4 cup milk

1/2 tsp salt

Dash pepper

Dash nutmeg

1 cup grated cheese (a mix of cheddar, Swiss or any cheeses of your choice)

3–4 thin slices of ham, broken in pieces

2 tbsp butter (cut into pea-size dots)

Partially bake the pie shell (about 10 minutes). Beat the eggs, cream and milk. Add seasonings, cheese and ham. Pour into the partially baked pie shell. Put pieces of butter on top. Bake in a preheated 350°F oven for 30–45 minutes until the egg mixture is set.

Serves 6–8

Orange French Toast

4 eggs

2 cups orange juice

1/2 tsp salt

1 tbsp sugar

24 slices day-old bread

6 tbsp butter or margarine

Beat the eggs, orange juice, salt and sugar together. Dip the bread into the egg mixture, coating both sides. Place bread slices in a well-greased shallow baking dish. Melt butter (or margarine) and drizzle over the bread. Bake in a hot (450°F) oven for 5 minutes. Turn and bake until golden (about 5–7 minutes). Serve with Orange Syrup.

Makes 12 servings (2 slices per serving)

Orange Syrup

2 cups light corn syrup

2 tsp grated orange peel

1/2 cup orange juice

Combine the 3 ingredients and simmer 5 minutes. Serve warm over Orange French Toast slices.

Southern Chicken Salad

1 head romaine lettuce
3 cups shredded cooked chicken
3/4 cup ripe olives, halved
1/3 cup sunflower seeds
1/4 lb whole green beans
Cherry tomatoes, ripe olives (sliced), sunflower seeds (to garnish)
Mustard Dressing (see below)

Line a salad bowl with lettuce leaves. Shred the remaining lettuce and put in the bowl. Combine chicken, olives, sunflower seeds and 1/2 cup Mustard Dressing. Heap chicken salad over the shredded lettuce. Steam green beans until tender; drain. Arrange green beans on top of the chicken salad. Garnish with cherry tomatoes, ripe olives (sliced) and sunflower seeds. Serve with extra dressing.

Serves 6

Mustard Dressing

Combine 1/3 cup white wine vinegar, 1 tbsp Dijon mustard, 5 tsp sugar, 2 cloves garlic (minced) and 1/4 tsp salt in a blender until smooth. Continue blending while slowly adding 1/2 cup vegetable oil until blended and dressing is thickened.

Makes 1 cup

Spring! Ah, the sound of the word makes the heart dance and sing. Spring!

Hearts of Palm Salad

6 cups torn fresh spinach

1 small carrot, shredded

1/2 cup oil and vinegar salad dressing

1/4 tsp dried oregano, crushed

1 14-oz can hearts of palm, drained, sliced and chilled

Fresh parsley, fresh oregano sprigs (optional)

Toss together spinach and carrot. Cover and chill. Combine salad dressing and oregano in a screw-top jar. Cover and shake to combine. Chill. Before serving, place spinach and carrot mix in a salad bowl. Top with hearts of palm. Drizzle dressing mixture over the salad. Garnish with parsley and oregano sprigs if desired. Serve immediately.

Serves 6 as a meal course—more as a brunch

Yogurt Lemon Nut Cake

3 tsp grated lemon peel, divided

1/2 cup finely chopped walnuts

1 cup plus 2 tbsp sugar, divided

1 cup butter or margarine, softened

4 eggs

1 1/2 tsp vanilla extract

2 1/2 cups all-purpose flour

1/2 tsp salt

1 tsp baking powder

1 tsp baking soda

1 cup plain yogurt

Glaze:

1/4 cup lemon juice

1/4 cup sugar

Preheat oven to 350°F. Grease 9 x 13-inch baking pan. In a small bowl combine 1 tsp lemon peel, walnuts and 2 tbsp sugar; set aside. In a large mixer bowl cream butter or margarine and 1 cup sugar until light and fluffy. Add eggs one at a time, beating well after each addition. Add remaining 2 tsp lemon peel and vanilla. In a medium bowl combine flour, salt, baking powder and baking soda. With mixer at low speed add dry ingredients alternately with yogurt, beginning and ending with dry ingredients. Spread evenly into pan. Sprinkle lemon–walnut mixture over the batter. Bake 30 minutes or until a toothpick inserted in the centre comes out clean. Let cool 10 minutes.

Glaze: In a small saucepan combine lemon juice and sugar. Heat to boiling, stirring until sugar dissolves. Pour hot glaze slowly over warm cake.

Serves 24

Edna's Household Hints

- When softened butter or margarine is needed in a hurry, just grate the amount needed using a coarse grater. The small grated pieces of butter or margarine will soften quickly at room temperature.

- If roasted nuts lose their crispness when stored in the refrigerator (where they should be), you can freshen them in a hurry by heating them in a low oven until they are just crisp.

- Vinegar is excellent for removing calcium deposits in a teakettle. Fill the kettle half full with a mixture of one-half vinegar, one-half water (or full-strength vinegar if deposits are really bad). Boil for about ten minutes, remove from heat, let cool, swirl it around as you pour it out, then rinse the kettle very well. For particularly stubborn deposits, let the vinegar mixture sit overnight once you've boiled it. Rinse well in the morning.

- To keep your sink drain clean and odour-free, pour in 1/2 cup baking soda and 1 cup white vinegar. Wait until it foams up, flush well with hot water, then cold. This should be done monthly.

- Company popping in and you have dishes in the sink? Load them in a plastic dishpan and put the pan in the oven (cold of course).

*Two proud young women in their crisp
nurse's uniforms.*

May

I wandered lonely as a cloud
That floats on high o'er vales and hills,
When all at once I saw a crowd,
A host of golden daffodils;
Beside the lake, beneath the trees,
Fluttering and dancing in the breeze.

—William Wordsworth

When I was very young, a teacher in our school had the class memorize that poem. It was just another piece of memory work until Miss Marsh, an inspired teacher, took us outdoors for a walk. She led us down the road and through the field of a neighbouring farm to the pond. Along the edge of the pond were hundreds of daffodils in full bloom waving in the gentle breeze. "Lie down on your stomachs," she ordered us, and there with our chins resting on our hands we listened to her recite the words of Wordsworth. His poem took on real meaning as her melodic voice rang out: "A host of golden daffodils." I think that my love of poetry began on that day, and I can still close my eyes and see those beautiful yellow blooms as they waved beside the Jacksons' pond.

The month of May provides us with rhubarb, whose tender shoots can be utilized in so many ways: rhubarb pies, tarts, punch, puddings and marmalades, to name but a few. Wherever we lived we always designated one section of our garden to rhubarb. We started our first rhubarb from plants that we dug up from my grandmother's garden. As youngsters we would pull some of the first tender stalks from the garden, give them a quick wash at the outdoor pump and then go directly to the sugar bowl on Grandma's kitchen table. There we would sit dipping the ends of the stalks in sugar, biting off the sugared piece and then dipping again. If Grandma thought this practice unsanitary, she never said a word. Later on, Grandma was so pleased to help George and me start our own rhubarb patch with plants from her garden.

From our families, friends and neighbours in the many parishes in which we lived, I have compiled some of my favourite rhubarb recipes to share with you.

Mother McCann's Rhubarb and Raspberry Jam

4 cups rhubarb, chopped

3 cups raspberries

4 cups sugar

Put rhubarb in a pot with water to cover. Bring water to a boil and simmer until rhubarb is soft. Drain, rinse and drain again. Add raspberries and bring to a boil. Add sugar and cook until thickened, stirring all the time. Seal in sterilized sealer jars.

Yields about 6 pints

Rhubarb Punch

8 cups sliced rhubarb

5 cups water

2 cups sugar (approx)

6 oranges

3 lemons

1 large-size plastic bottle ginger ale, chilled

Simmer the rhubarb in the water until it is very mushy (about 15 minutes). Strain. Measure the liquid and add about 1/3 cup sugar for each cup of liquid, stirring over heat until sugar has dissolved. Cool. Add the juice of the oranges and the lemons. Chill. Just before serving add the ginger ale. Serve over ice cubes.

Makes 1 large punch bowl

If your rhubarb is red, the punch will have a lovely pink colour (if it isn't you may add a drop or two of red food colouring).

When selecting rhubarb you should know that the darker red the stalk, the more pungent the flavour—pink rhubarb has a milder taste.

Rhubarb Pie

1 tbsp butter
1 1/4 cups sugar
2 cups diced rhubarb
2 egg yolks
1 tbsp flour
1 8-inch baked pie shell
4 tbsp sugar
2 egg whites

Melt butter, add 1 cup of the sugar and all of the rhubarb, cook until the rhubarb is slightly softened and the sugar melted. Add slightly beaten egg yolks. Mix the remaining 1/4 cup of sugar with flour and add to rhubarb mixture. Cook until rhubarb is of jelly-like consistency. Pour into baked pie shell and top with meringue made by gradually beating sugar into beaten egg whites. Brown in a 300°F oven about 15 minutes.

Edna's Preserving Tips

When making jams, jellies or relishes it is important to use sterilized jars and lids. Thankfully, the newer Mason jars have self-sealing metal "dome" lids with a rubber-like sealing compound around the edge where the lid meets the rim of the jar; the lid is held in place with a metal screw band. *Note:* You never re-use the flat lids as the sealing compound loses its original muscle—you'll use fresh lids for each canning session.

Carefully check your jars and discard any with nicked, cracked or chipped rims. All jars and lids should be washed in hot soapy water. Rinse thoroughly with hot water. Sterilize the jars by covering them with water and boiling them for 15 minutes. Let them wait in the sterilizing water to keep hot until you fill them.

Do not boil the self-sealing lids as boiling hurts their ability to seal. Instead, put them in a bowl, cover them with briskly boiling water and let them stand until ready to use.

EACH YEAR ABOUT THIS time my son-in-law Bruce comes into the kitchen and announces that it is "Diet time! My summer slacks don't fit!" I'm sure that this pronouncement is made in kitchens everywhere and often the month of May is "light eating" for many of us hoping to be able to wear last year's summer clothing.

To get a start on this calorie cutback, here are two light-eating recipes that are delicious but low in fat.

Pasta Primavera

5 oz corkscrew macaroni or fettuccini noodles

1/4 cup water

2 cups sliced fresh mushrooms

1 9-oz pkg frozen French-style green beans

1/2 cup coarsely chopped green or sweet red pepper (or combination of the two)

1 clove garlic, minced

Salt and pepper to taste

1 12-oz can evaporated skim milk

4 tsp cornstarch

1/2 cup shredded mozzarella cheese (provolone cheese may be used)

1 medium tomato, cut into wedges

Cook pasta according to package directions; drain well.

While pasta is cooking: In a medium saucepan combine 1/4 cup water, mushrooms, frozen green beans, green or red pepper, garlic, salt and pepper. Bring to a boil, then reduce heat. Cover and simmer 4 minutes or until vegetables are tender. Do not drain. Stir together milk and cornstarch; stir into vegetable mixture. Cook over medium heat until thickened and bubbly. Cook and stir for 1 minute more. Add cheese, stir until melted. To serve, pour sauce over pasta. Garnish with tomato wedges.

Serves 4

Pineapple Chicken and Rice Bake

2 lb meaty chicken pieces (breasts, thighs and drumsticks), skinned

1/2 cup chopped onion

1 large red sweet pepper, cut into 3/4-inch squares

1 8-oz can pineapple chunks (undrained, packed in juice)

1/4 cup frozen orange juice concentrate, thawed

2 tbsp soy sauce

1/8 tsp ground cloves

2/3 cup long-grain rice

1 cup chicken broth

Parsley sprigs or paprika for garnish

Place chicken pieces, onion and red pepper into a large sealable plastic bag set in a deep bowl. In a small mixing bowl stir together undrained pineapple, orange juice concentrate, soy sauce and cloves. Pour pineapple mixture into the bag with the chicken. Seal the bag. Place bag in bowl in the refrigerator to marinate the chicken for 4–24 hours, turning the bag occasionally.

Before baking, drain the chicken, reserving marinade and vegetables. Set chicken aside. Place uncooked rice in a 12 x 7 1/2 x 2-inch baking dish. Stir chicken broth and the reserved marinade–vegetable mixture into the rice. Top with chicken pieces. Cover with foil. Bake in a preheated 375°F oven about 1 hour or until chicken and rice are tender. Garnish with parsley or sprinkle with paprika.

Serves 6

*My husband George was never fond of dieting.
After a particularly trying week of low-calorie foods
and small portions, he announced, "I am giving up
dieting. If anyone asks about my weight tell them
I'm on a special government assignment—fat-testing
for the military."*

HERE IN CANADA THE month of May provides us with the Victoria Day holiday. Queen Victoria, the late British monarch, was born on May 24, 1819. A very young woman when she became queen, she was the longest reigning monarch in British history. Her common sense and direct-ness of character made her beloved by her subjects and brought the British nation to its place of prominence in the world. As a member nation of the Commonwealth we have celebrated Victoria's birthday on the Monday closest to her birth date and this holiday weekend gives cottage owners a chance to open the cottage and ready it for the summer to come.

For years Marg, Bruce and I have spent this holiday week-end in Muskoka helping my good friend Eleanor open her cottage. Many years ago, after Eleanor's husband passed away, she was concerned about coming to the cottage alone. Bob had done all of the larger physical jobs. He turned on the power and the water, checking pipes for cracks and leaks. He gave the deck chairs a fresh coat of paint and he put the boat in the water after he had adjusted the engine. The thought of coming north and facing this alone was overwhelming. When Bruce told her he would be happy to lend his handy-man skills, Eleanor was thrilled. Now, each holiday weekend is spent seeing to the multitude of small but important jobs that ensure a happy, work-free summer. After a day's work at the cottage it's good to sit down to an early supper.

On this weekend in particular it's nice to have a supper dish that can be made ahead of time, and served with a crisp salad and a minimum of fuss.

Beef and Sausage Lasagna

1/2 lb hot Italian sausage links

1/2 lb ground beef

1 medium onion, diced

1 28-oz can Italian plum tomatoes

2 tbsp tomato paste

1 tsp salt

1 tsp sugar

3/4 tsp Italian seasoning

2/3 16-oz pkg lasagna noodles (about 12 noodles)

1 16-oz container part-skim ricotta cheese

1 large egg

1/4 cup chopped parsley

1 8-oz pkg shredded part-skim mozzarella cheese

Remove sausage from casings. In a 4-quart saucepan over high heat, cook sausage meat, ground beef and onion, stirring frequently until meat is well browned and onion is tender, stirring to break up sausage. Spoon off any fat. Add tomatoes with their liquid, tomato paste, salt, sugar and Italian seasoning; heat to boiling. Reduce heat to low, cover and simmer 30 minutes, stirring occasionally. While sauce is cooking, prepare lasagna noodles as package directs but do not salt the water. Drain.

In a bowl mix ricotta cheese, egg and parsley. In a 13 x 9-inch glass baking dish arrange half of the lasagna noodles; top with all of the ricotta mixture. Sprinkle with half of mozzarella; top with half of meat sauce. Layer with remaining noodles and meat sauce; top with remaining mozzarella. Cover lasagna with foil. Refrigerate until ready to bake. Preheat oven to 375°F. Bake covered lasagna for about 30 minutes. Remove foil and bake 15 minutes longer or until lasagna is hot and bubbly and top is lightly browned. Remove lasagna from oven; let stand for 10 minutes for easier serving.

Serves 8–10

Serve with a green salad and hot bread, and you have an easy delicious dinner that's perfect for a cottage work weekend.

THE VICTORIA DAY WEEKEND is also the time when many people bring out their barbeques. Jake Frampton, an old friend, has taken a cooking course and has become quite a chef. He has offered to share some of his favourite barbeque recipes.

Barbequed Back Ribs

Pork back ribs (approx 1 lb per person)
Your favourite barbeque sauce

Jake says that the secret of tender, juicy barbequed ribs is in the precooking.

Cut ribs in sections of 4–5 ribs. Arrange ribs in a roasting pan and generously cover with barbeque sauce. Seal the pan with foil and place in a preheated 225°F oven. Precook ribs for 3 1/2–4 hours. Check every half hour to be sure that there is enough sauce to keep the ribs moist. Heat the barbeque and move the ribs from the roasting pan to the grill. Baste the ribs with sauce and grill just long enough to crisp the sauce. Do not overcook.

Barbequed Fish Fillets

Put fish fillets in foil. Sprinkle with garlic salt, melted butter and lemon juice. Seal the fish in the foil. Grill on the barbeque until fish is flaky (approx 20 minutes).

Mixed Fruit

Cut fresh fruit in chunks or slices and marinate for 2 hours in a mixture of kirsch and honey. Arrange fruit on skewers and broil over hot coals for 10 minutes. When done, sprinkle with lemon juice.

Climbing the shadowed pathway
No lovelier flower I see
Than the shy little violet,
Hiding modestly.
Months and days I've wasted
Doing some useless things
How few the hours that have been well spent
Viewing the flowers in Spring.

—Fujivara Okikaza

BY THE END OF May we have usually had many warm days. A few of these are hot enough that a cold drink poured over ice can be a welcome relief.

This recipe for Russian Tea has been used in our family for decades. It is easy to make and just a little different from plain iced tea or lemonade. The secret is the black tea. Black tea comes from Russia and its flavour is quite different from any other tea that I know. Black tea may not be readily available in all supermarkets, but most stores specializing in unusual teas and coffees will have black tea on hand.

Russian Tea

2 tbsp black tea

4 cups boiling water

1 cup sugar

Juice of 4 lemons

Pour boiling water over tea. Add sugar and lemon juice. Let stand 2 hours then strain through a cloth. Add ice, serve.

A lovely bride adorned with flowers.

June

And what is so rare as a day in June?
Then, if ever, come perfect days;
Then Heaven tries the earth if it be in tune,
And over it softly her warm ear lays.

—James Russell Lowell

In our area June really does seem to have more "perfect days" than the other months. Warmer days and nights than April or May but not the steamy or uncomfortable hot times of July and August make the thirty days of June some of the most enjoyable days of the year.

June is a very special month for me as I celebrate my birthday and the anniversary of my marriage. George and I were both very young when we made our vows so long ago. We were married in my father's church and if I close my eyes I can still see the handsome young man who waited for me at the front of the church as I walked nervously down the aisle on my father's arm. The bishop of our area was the presiding minister and we could not have asked for a lovelier day or a more beautiful service.

George and I had many happy years together and in his honour I offer this recipe for his favourite dessert. No matter what the weather, George was thrilled to see Chocolate Denver Pudding after any meal. Actually, he would have preferred this pudding as the entire meal.

Chocolate Denver Pudding

Mix first:

3/4 cup sugar

1 cup flour

1/8 tsp salt

2 tsp baking soda

2 tbsp butter

1 square semi-sweet chocolate or 3 tbsp cocoa

1/2 cup milk

1/2 tsp vanilla

Mix second (for the top):

1/2 cup brown sugar

1/2 cup white sugar

4 tbsp cocoa

1 1/2 cups cold water

In a bowl mix sugar, flour, salt and baking soda. Put butter and chocolate (or cocoa) in a small saucepan. Place saucepan in a larger pan of boiling water on the stovetop to melt the butter and chocolate. Add melted butter/chocolate to the flour mixture. Slowly add milk and vanilla and mix well to form batter. Pour batter into a well-greased 9 x 9-inch baking dish.

Mix together brown sugar, white sugar and cocoa. Scatter the mixture over the batter. Pour 1 1/2 cups water over the topping mixture. Bake in a preheated 350°F oven for 40 minutes.

Serves 6 (or 1 real chocolate lover)

THE SOON-TO-ARRIVE SUMMER is even more apparent as the early fruits and vegetables make their way to the stores and the outdoor Farmers' Markets. In our town the Farmers' Market opens on the long weekend in May and it remains open each weekend until the end of October. Main Street is blocked off each Saturday morning at 6:00 a.m. and the farmers from our area set up their stalls that feature fresh produce, meat, fish, cheese and a host of other "just-picked" fruits and vegetables. I like to get there early and enjoy a hot apple cider and bacon-on-a-bun for my breakfast. As well it gives me a chance to meet with my many friends and neighbours who also enjoy an early start to their day.

A dinner featuring those just-arrived delights is the perfect way to welcome the warmer days. When the beautiful weather outdoors begins to beckon us, it's nice to spend less time in the kitchen. Uncomplicated menus may become special with just a little flair—a salad with dandelion greens, or asparagus with Maltaise sauce—to remind you that spring is here and summer is just around the corner.

One of the nice things about looking for dandelion greens is that your neighbours are usually more than willing to donate any or all dandelions that are on their property. One of our former neighbours used to make dandelion wine. This meant that the lawns in our area were virtually weed free as Tony took advantage of the "generosity" of his neighbours to collect the weeds needed for his yearly bottling. Dandelion greens also make an unusual and delicious salad.

Dandelion Salad with Pine Nuts

1 1/2 lb dandelion greens, torn into 1/2-inch pieces,
*   washed and spun dry*
3 tbsp pine nuts (available in most markets' bulk food area)
1/4 cup extra virgin olive oil
1 1/2 tbsp red wine vinegar
Coarse salt
Freshly ground pepper

Mound the dandelion greens in a heat-proof salad bowl. In a small skillet cook the pine nuts in the olive oil over moderate heat, stirring, until they are golden. Hold the pan over the salad, remove the nuts with a slotted spoon and sprinkle them over the dandelion greens. Drizzle the hot oil over the greens quickly and toss until greens are covered. Sprinkle salad with the vinegar, salt and pepper to taste. Toss well.

Serves 6

MY GREAT-GRANDSON JUSTIN has his own opinion of asparagus. He feels that it should be left alone to grow in the field and that no one under the age of 37 should be made to eat it. It's an interesting assessment possibly shared by a number of youngsters, but not by those of us over 37. Here is one tasty recipe.

Asparagus with Maltaise Sauce

1 orange
1 large egg yolk
2 tsp fresh lemon juice
Pinch salt and white pepper (or to taste)
1/4 cup unsalted butter, melted and cooled
1 1/4 lb asparagus, trimmed and peeled

Blanch the orange, unpeeled, in a saucepan of boiling water
for 3 minutes. Drain off water and let orange cool. Grate the
rind finely and squeeze the orange for the juice (1 tsp).
Remaining juice may be reserved for another use. In a blender
or a food processor put the egg yolk, lemon juice, pinch of
salt and white pepper. Turn the machine on, then off immediately. Then with machine on, add butter in a steady stream.
Add grated rind and orange juice and blend until mixture is
well mixed. Transfer the sauce to a bowl and keep it warm,
covering the surface with a buttered round of waxed paper,
and set in a pan of warm water. Cook the asparagus in boiling
salted water 3–5 minutes until stalks are tender but not limp.
Drain well. Transfer the asparagus to a platter and serve it
with the sauce.

Serves 2 as a main course

WHILE WE ARE ENJOYING this delicious vegetable, we should give thanks to Diederick Teertower. He was the eighteenth-century Dutch consul for Massachusetts and New Hampshire who is credited with growing the first asparagus in America. It is said that he brought over some plants from Holland and successfully raised them in West Brookfield, Massachusetts. My favourite recipe for asparagus is delicious but simple.

Asparagus Amandine

2 lb asparagus, boiled

1/4 cup melted butter

1 tbsp grated onion

1/3 cup chopped (or sliced) almonds, browned

Salt and pepper

Place asparagus in shallow oven-proof dish. Mix butter and grated onion and pour over asparagus. Top with almonds. Put under broiler until the top browns slightly.

Serves 4

Love is the doorway through which the human soul passes from selfishness to service and from solitude to kinship with all mankind.

AT THIS TIME OF year one of the most delicious of fruits is ready to be picked. Is there anything that can beat the taste of a ripe red strawberry picked and eaten right in the field? Many farms in our area feature "pick your own" berries where visitors take their baskets into the field and select the choicest of the fruits to take home. One of the nicer benefits of the "pick your own" berry picking is that the farmers encourage berry "testing." Eating while picking will often encourage the very young pickers that you have with you.

The uses for strawberries seem to be nearly limitless. I have included some of the recipes that our family has enjoyed for years as well as a few that have come to us from the newer family members.

Strawberry Ice Cream

4 cups strawberries

1 cup sugar

4 cups cream

Crush strawberries and stir in sugar. Chill. Add cream, mix and freeze.

Makes about 8 cups

Strawberry Custard

4 eggs

1/4 cup sugar

1/8 tsp salt

1 cup scalded milk

1 tsp vanilla

1 cup whipping cream

2 cups strawberries, washed and chilled

Separate the eggs. Beat egg yolks slightly, then add sugar and salt. Stir in the scalded milk slowly and cook over very low heat until custard begins to thicken. Stir in vanilla and let cool. When ready to serve, whip the cream and fold in beaten egg whites. Fold in the custard and strawberries.

Serves 4

THE MONTH OF JUNE was a very busy one in the life of a minister and his family. Along with the many weddings that traditionally occurred in June, there were two very important social events that happened. One was the "Church Picnic" and the other was the "Strawberry Social." In most small parishes, the "Strawberry Social" was (and often still is) a marvellous fundraiser. The ladies of the church set up long tables, covered them with sparkling white sheets (which they called tablecloths) and set about serving the best strawberry shortcake ever made. Sometimes it was served as dessert at the end of a chicken dinner (also prepared by the ladies of the church) but often people chose to make a meal of the shortcake and berries.

The Strawberry Shortcake recipe that we used most often included Baking Powder Biscuits because it was easier to make up individual servings than to bake large cakes and have to cut them into pieces. Here is our "country social" version of this classic dessert.

Strawberry Shortcake

8 cups strawberries
Sugar to taste, usually 1 1/2–2 cups
1 1/2 cups whipping cream

About 2 hours before serving time, hull and slice the strawberries into a large bowl. Sugar them to taste and let them sit, turning occasionally. Half an hour before serving time, put the bowl for whipping the cream and the beaters in the refrigerator to chill. Mix up the Baking Powder Biscuits and put in the oven. Five minutes before the biscuits are done, whip the cream.

Baking Powder Biscuits

2 cups flour
4 tsp baking powder
1 tsp salt
2 tbsp sugar
2 tbsp shortening
3/4 cup milk, approx

Mix flour, baking powder, salt and sugar, and sift together twice. Cut in the shortening with 2 knives or a pastry blender. Mix in milk gradually to make a soft dough. Sometimes you may need a little more milk. Roll out dough on a floured board to 1/2-inch thick and cut with a biscuit cutter or the top of a juice glass. Arrange the rounds of dough on a greased baking sheet and bake at 450°F for 12–15 minutes, removing when the biscuits begin to brown on top. To serve, put the bowls of strawberries and whipped cream and a basket of hot biscuits on the table and let everyone make their own.

THE "CHURCH PICNIC" PROVIDED the members of the parish, particularly the youngsters, with a chance to enjoy a day of organized games and a delicious meal with family and good friends. Three-legged races, sack races, tug-o'-war and pie-eating contests were all part of the fun. George, the girls and I were active participants in the festivities. Julia, the competitive member of our family, often convinced her sisters that practice was the best way to win any of the events and she would talk them into "training" for weeks ahead of the picnic. Usually the girls acquitted themselves well but, in all honesty, I think that Mary and Marg did so because they didn't want to have to listen to Julia's dissertation on their short-comings if they didn't live up to her expectations.

It seems picnic food has changed very little over the years—sandwiches of egg salad, ham, tuna or salmon salad along with potato salad, relish trays and large thermoses of lemonade have been travelling in large wicker baskets to pic-nic sites for decades. Nearly every family has their own spe-cial potato salad recipe and ours has changed very little since my grandmother first made it so many years ago.

Grandmother MacIntosh's Potato Salad

4 cups boiled potatoes, diced
2 hard-boiled eggs, sliced
1 onion, minced
1/2 cup olives, chopped
1/2 cup celery, diced
1/4 cup celery leaves, minced
1/4 cup radishes, sliced
1/2 cup cucumber, diced
Salt, pepper and fresh dill to taste
1 1/2 cups mayonnaise
Paprika

In a large bowl mix first 10 ingredients. Just before serving sprinkle with paprika. (Fresh dill adds a little zip to the salad but children often prefer it without.)

Serves 8–10

Beauty is not immortal. In a day blossom and June
and rapture pass away.

—Arthur Stringer

Another very popular addition to picnic fare is good old-fashioned Fried Chicken.

Fried Chicken

12–16 small chicken pieces
Salt and pepper
1/4 cup quick-mix flour
1 egg, lightly beaten
1/2 cup bread crumbs
4 tbsp butter
1 tbsp oil

Wipe and dry the chicken pieces. Sprinkle pieces with a little salt and pepper. Place the flour, egg and bread crumbs in three separate shallow bowls. Coat the chicken lightly with flour, dip to coat with egg, and finally, roll in bread crumbs. Cover the pieces with waxed paper and refrigerate until cooking time.

To cook: Sauté the breaded chicken pieces in a skillet over medium-high heat in the butter and oil mixture. Fry until golden brown. Do the pieces in batches so that the pan is not crowded and add more butter if needed. Remove chicken from pan and allow to drain on paper towels. Serve hot or cold with lemon wedges and chopped parsley.

OUR FRENCH CANADIAN FRIENDS honour their patron saint on a very special day in the month of June. St. Jean Baptiste Day, June 24th, is celebrated with unbridled enthusiasm in the province of Québec.

One of the most popular dishes enjoyed by the Québecois is the traditional Tortière. Madeleine Pouliot, a friend living in Québec City, sends along her recipe.

Tortière

In a pot mix together 1/2 lb each lean ground beef and ground pork.

Add:

1 onion, chopped

1 clove garlic, minced

1/2 tsp salt

1/2 tsp savory or thyme

1/4 tsp celery salt

1/4 tsp ground cloves

1/2 cup water

Bring all ingredients to a boil. Turn down to simmer for 20 minutes. Add 1/2 cup breadcrumbs spoon by spoon until the fat is absorbed. Cool mixture. Pour into uncooked pie shell. Add the top crust. Cook 25 minutes in a preheated 450°F oven.

MY DEAR FRIEND MADELEINE was born and raised
in Québec City. She was married at a young age to Dr. Paul
Pouliot, a Québec City physician, and they became the par-
ents of five children. I was in awe of this lovely lady! As well
as a house in the city the family owned a large cottage on Île
d'Orléans and, for winter skiing, a chalet at Lac Beauport.
On any weekend, in any season, two or three of Paul's broth-
ers, their wives and their families would spend the weekend
with Paul and Madeleine. This meant that serving meals for
24–30 people was the norm. Madeleine simply took all this in
her stride and I never ever heard her complain. The secret to
her successful management was her marvellous organiza-
tional skills. Children as young as three or four years of age
would help set the table and each older child would have
some chore that would ensure that a delicious, nutritious
meal would be served to all. I freely admit that I envied
Madeleine's serenity and calm in the midst of what I often
thought was chaos.

Another of Madeleine's delicious recipes is Poulet à la
mode de Roquefort, or Chicken with Roquefort Cheese.

Chicken with Roquefort Cheese

2 1-1/2-lb broilers, split
Salt and pepper to taste
3 tbsp butter
6 oz Roquefort cheese
1 clove garlic, minced
1 1/2 cups sour cream

Rub the broilers with the salt and pepper. Melt the butter in
a skillet. Brown the chickens in the skillet; remove and arrange
in a baking dish. Mash the cheese with a fork. Blend with
the garlic and sour cream. Spread over the chicken. Cover.
Bake in a 375°F oven until the chicken is tender, about
30 minutes, removing the cover for the last 5 minutes.

Serves 4

Cooling off on a hot summer day.

July

July, to me, is summer at its best. The days are hot and sunny, evenings warm enough to sit out until the moon and stars make their appearance. The pace of life slows down and there seems to be more time to enjoy our friends and our family. When our girls were young, July was the month that George had as his vacation. For many years George would offer to replace other vacationing ministers in various parishes in cottage country. Our accommodation was supplied, usually a small cottage on the lake, and it meant that the girls, George and I had a wonderful chance to relax, swim, fish and spend time with each other. George would preach at Sunday morning services but the rest of the time was his to enjoy.

We were lucky enough to go to the same parish for a number of summers. This meant that we made several close friends in the area and the girls had many other youngsters with whom they could enjoy the simple joys and pleasures of summer at the lake. Some of these cottage friends remain close to this day.

"Canada Day," July 1st, celebrates the birth of our nation back in 1867. With the signing of the Articles of Confederation, this magnificent country called Canada came into being. In 1967 we celebrated our one hundredth birthday with an extravagant show of patriotism marked by much flag-waving and brilliant displays of fireworks.

July 1st is a wonderful time to have a get-together with an easy dinner menu, so that everyone can enjoy the holiday. A simple dinner will give the cook lots of time to sit and visit with the guests. After dinner, if paper plates are used, there is almost no cleanup involved and everyone can sit back and enjoy the fireworks that have become a part of Canada Day celebrations everywhere.

To start off the dinner, here is a refreshing cool soup that needs no cooking.

Chilled Cucumber Parsley Soup

1 cup natural yogurt

2 cups light cream or 1 cup milk and 1 cup heavy cream

2 medium seedless cucumbers, peeled and chopped

1 cup fresh parsley

1/3 cup finely chopped chives or green onions

2 tsp salt

Stir yogurt and cream together until smooth. Stir in remaining ingredients and refrigerate until serving time. Garnish with thin unpeeled cucumber slices and a dash of paprika.

Serves 6

Rolled Rib Roast

Bind one 6–8-lb rolled rib roast with a heavy string or butcher's cord. Place on spit, securing with prongs. Turn spit constantly over low to medium heat on a gas barbeque. Baste with a barbeque sauce of your choice. Barbeque until meat is at desired doneness. Cool before carving.

Cheesy Potato Fingers

6 medium-size potatoes
4 tbsp butter
Salt and pepper
Chopped parsley
3/4 cup grated sharp cheddar cheese
1/2 cup light cream

Peel the potatoes and cut as for french fries. Using a double sheet of foil shaped as a pan, place potatoes in the centre of the foil. Dot the potatoes with butter. Sprinkle with salt and pepper, parsley and cheese. Pour cream over the potatoes and close the foil to seal tightly. Place foil pan on the rack of the barbeque on high heat for 40–50 minutes. Turn at half time to ensure that the potatoes cook evenly. If you are cooking meat on the barbeque at a lower heat, potatoes may be oven cooked. Place the foil pan on a cookie sheet in a 425°F oven for 40–50 minutes.

A salad adds a nice touch to the dinner and saves preparing other vegetables. Hearts of romaine make a good substitute for the elegant (and expensive) Belgian endive. Add avocado and mushrooms, serve with a vinaigrette dressing, and you have a salad fit for a Canada Day celebration.

If your family is like mine, dessert is an essential part of any special dinner. While I would be happy with a serving of fresh fruit, the rest of the family will be looking for something sweet and delicious. This next recipe for Berries and Cream seems to fill the bill for all of us, and as well it gives a touch of patriotic red and white.

Berries and Cream

4 cups strawberries

4 cups red raspberries

1/3 cup sugar

1 cup heavy cream

1/4 cup sugar

Divide strawberries among 6 serving dishes. In a blender or food processor, purée the raspberries with 1/3 cup sugar. Whip cream, sweetening with remaining sugar. Pour the raspberry purée over the strawberries and garnish with a dollop of whipped cream.

Yellow butterflies
Over the blossoming virgin corn
With pollen-painted faces
Chase one another in brilliant throng.

—A Hopi song

THIS MONTH IS ALSO a time of celebration in the United States. Americans are unabashedly and unapologetically proud of being American and "The Glorious Fourth" gives them the opportunity to shout it from the rooftops! George and I were lucky enough (on several occasions) to spend the Fourth of July holiday with friends in New England. The year that I remember best we were on Cape Cod, the beautiful cape in southern Massachusetts that is the summer home of many of Boston's wealthiest and most influential families. We were invited to a clambake, a feast that has changed little since the days when the natives on the continent used the clams in seaside celebrations.

A "proper" clambake starts off with Clam Chowder.

Clam Chowder

4 cups shucked clams

1/4 lb salt pork, diced

2 onions, finely sliced

6 medium-size potatoes, sliced thin

1/2 tsp salt

1/8 tsp pepper

4 cups milk

2 tbsp butter

Rinse clams in clam liquor. Remove black caps. Strain and reserve 1/2 cup clam liquor. Chop clams and set aside. Fry salt pork until brown and crisp. Drain on paper reserving 1 tsp fat. Sauté onion slices, then add potatoes. Sprinkle with salt and pepper. Sauté for 10 minutes. Add chopped clams and 1/2 cup clam liquor. Cover with water and cook for 20 minutes. Add fried pork and fat to clams and vegetables. Then heat milk and add to the chowder. Add butter, season to taste and serve.

Serves 8

Clam Broth, made as described below, is served as an accompaniment to the rest of the "bake."

Clam Broth

4 cups clams
2 cups cold water

Scrub clams and rinse several times until free from sand. Place clams in a large kettle, add water and cover. Cook over low heat for 20 minutes. Remove clams from broth. Let stand so that liquor can settle. Strain. Serve hot or cold.

A REAL NEW ENGLAND clambake starts early in the afternoon. Roundish stones about a foot in diameter are placed to cover a circular area about three feet in diameter. A good hot fire is then built on top of the stones and the fire is kept roaring for about two hours. Stones will be white hot by this time. Coals and ashes are raked away and the stones are covered with a six-inch layer of rockweed—a type of seaweed that contains small air bubbles.

Quart-size bags of cheesecloth are filled with clams, potatoes, sweet corn (husks removed) or lobsters. It's important to tie the bags low enough to leave a handle for when it comes time to remove them from the hot seaweed. The corn and the lobsters are placed on the first layer of rockweed. The food bags are then covered with rockweed and the bags of clams and potatoes are laid on top. Over all of this is laid a sheet of wet canvas, which is kept wet for the next forty-five minutes of baking.

Really, this is just a rather interesting way of steaming food, but the salt and herby steam that come from the rockweed add a delicious flavour not otherwise possible.

AS THE DAYS GET hotter it's nice to spend time in the garden reading in the shade of a large willow tree. I have always loved to read! My father encouraged this love by reading to us every night and by being certain that good books were always available when we were able to read on our own. Although I enjoy mysteries and have probably read every mystery book ever written, my favourite authors are humourists. I believe the best book that I have ever read was written by that wonderul Canadian humourist, Stephen Leacock. *Sunshine Sketches of a Little Town* is so Canadian and so brilliantly written that if you have not read it you should make yourself a cold drink and take it and the book to your favourite reading chair and enjoy!

Lila MacGuiness, an old friend and neighbour, gave me this recipe to share with you.

Egg Colada

1 12-oz can colada mix

1 cup crushed pineapple

Juice of 1/2 lemon or lime

6 ice cubes

4 eggs

Place all ingredients in a blender or food processor and blend. Pour into tall glasses and garnish with fresh pineapple pieces. Serve immediately. (Never use cracked eggs in this recipe.)

Makes 4 1/2 cups

My daughter Julia uses this recipe in very hot weather when she wants to keep cool—and stay slim.

Blueberry Cooler

1/2 cup skim milk

1/2 cup blueberries (fresh or frozen)

1/2 cup ice cubes

1 cup diet ginger ale

Blend milk, blueberries and ice for 30 seconds in a blender, then pour into tall glasses. Add ginger ale and stir.

Serves 2

*I cannot imagine a pleasanter old age than one spent
in the not too remote country where I could re-read
and annotate my favourite books.*

—*André Maurois*

A SUMMER ACTIVITY OFTEN enjoyed by our daughters Marg, Mary and Julia was that of selling lemonade from a home-made stand. The three of them persuaded George to build a wooden kiosk, which they painted a rather spectacular shade of green. Many a hot summer's day would find the girls perched on stools behind the counter purveying this cooling drink for two cents per glass. Our neighbours, bless their hearts, were sure to stop and buy at least one glass each and many times they would enjoy a refill, much to the delight of the girls who were always saving for some special treat or another.

Lemonade is not just a thirst quencher; it is a drink that brings back some wonderful memories of summer days gone by. For me, nothing can take the place of an icy cold glass of lemonade. Although many people these days buy premixed lemonade in large quantities, I much prefer to make my own. This recipe is simple but delicious.

Lemonade

12 lemons
1 1/4 cups sugar
12 cups spring water
Mint sprigs

Lemons should be at room temperature. Roll the lemons to soften. Squeeze the lemons into a 4-quart container, carefully removing the pips but not the pulp. Add sugar and water. Stir well to dissolve the sugar. Taste and add more sugar if desired. Chill very well. When serving, pour over ice and add mint sprigs.

Serves 12

WHEN THE FAMILY GETS together for a barbeque dinner, is there anything more popular than the hamburger? These days the hamburger has evolved into a gourmet delight—blue cheese, mushrooms, pineapple or guacamole are just a few of the toppings that have turned the once ordinary burger into an entrée that is welcomed even in the finest and most well-to-do homes.

My grandson Marshall makes a terrific burger but it's not really possible to give you the exact recipe. This isn't because he wouldn't like to share it, but because he never measures his ingredients and so each batch of burgers is different. He has given me a list of ingredients that he uses, so perhaps you would like to experiment with them to see if you too can produce a "beautiful burger" that the family raves about.

Marshall's Burger

2 lb medium ground beef
1 egg

Worcestershire sauce

Soya sauce

Teriyaki sauce

Minced or chopped garlic

Barbeque sauce (mixed in, and brushed on while cooking;
Hickory-smoked sauce is the favourite of our family)

Combine all ingredients. Pack the meat into good-size patties and barbeque to desired doneness.

My granddaughter Phyllis's favourite burger recipe comes from her friend Christie. It is a Hawaiian Burger that features—what else—pineapple slices.

Christie's Hawaiian Burger

2 lb ground beef

1/2 cup finely chopped onion

2 tsp salt

1/4 tsp pepper

2 eggs

Combine all ingredients, mixing well. Shape into 8 patties.

Sauce:

3 tbsp prepared mustard

3 tbsp ketchup

1 1/2 tbsp soy sauce

8 pineapple slices

Barbeque the hamburger patties over direct heat 10–15 minutes, basting with the sauce. After turning the burgers, top each with a pineapple slice. Serve on fresh buns.

A lovely morn!
The summer night is gone;
How hushed and still is all the world
Is wonder at the dawn.

—*Anonymous*

Snuggling on Grandfather's knee.

August

A few years ago my family and I took advantage of the Civic Holiday on the first Monday in August to enjoy a summer picnic. We spent the day on Toronto's Centre Island, a place I don't visit nearly often enough. We parked downtown and joined the throng of people in line to board the ferry. Once on the island, we walked the trails, watched as young children enjoyed the rides and the animal petting zoo, and then we found our perfect picnic area. It was a picnic table in the shade of a large tree with a lovely view of the lake. It was dusk when we caught the ferry to the city. The skyline of Toronto was a magnificent sight with which to end a delightful day.

Sometimes we forget that we have so many beautiful places to visit in this country. Toronto's Centre Island is certainly one of those places.

Summer afternoon—summer afternoon; to me those have always been the two most beautiful words in the English language.

—Henry James

IN THE SUMMER, WHETHER at home or at the cottage, friends and neighbours will often drop over in the evening. Sometimes they will stop just to sit and talk.

Occasionally a game of cards will occupy a few of the sunset hours. Often, though, we'll spend hours just sitting and watching the stars. If you are living or visiting outside of the city, stargazing is at its best at this time of year with spectacular displays of meteor showers or northern lights highly visible in the inky sky.

On these occasions it's nice to have something delicious but easy to make to serve with tea or coffee. The next two recipes will help you be a perfect summer hostess.

Summertime Squares

1/2 cup butter

1 cup shredded processed cheese (not cheddar)

1 1/2 cups flour

1 tsp baking powder

2 tbsp sugar

1 cup apple jelly

Cream together butter and cheese until thoroughly blended. Mix in flour, baking powder and sugar until batter is smooth. Press half of the mixture into an 8 x 8-inch pan. Cover evenly with the jelly and then cover with the remaining mixture. Bake in a preheated 325°F oven for 25 minutes. Cool and cut into squares.

Cheese Dreams

1 loaf unsliced white sandwich bread
Kraft Cheese Whiz (or other spreadable cheese)
8 slices bacon

Cut the crust off the bread. Cut the bread into 16 3 x 2 x 1-inch rectangles. Spread the Cheese Whiz on the 4 sides and top of each of the bread rectangles. Place on a cookie sheet. Partially cook the bacon and blot on paper towel to remove excess grease. Cut the bacon slices in half and place the half slices on top of the cheese-covered bread. Place the cookie sheet on the upper oven rack. Broil for 3–4 minutes or until the bacon is cooked and the cheese is bubbling and slightly browned. Serve immediately.

No one should make such thorough preparations for the rainy days that he cannot enjoy today's sunshine.

SOMETIMES AT THIS TIME of year we have a spell of rainy weather. Some people will tell you that if it rains on July 15th, St. Swithin's Day, it will rain for at least forty days. The story behind this superstition is interesting. When St. Swithin died, he had asked that he not be buried inside the cathedral but rather that he be laid to rest somewhere outside to be nearer to his parishioners. Unhappily, his instructions were not followed and he was buried inside the church. Several centuries later, it was decided that his wishes should have been honoured and his remains were removed to a grave outside by a walkway under the eaves of the cathedral. Legend has it that on the day of his reburial it rained in torrents and kept on doing so for weeks and weeks. Thus St. Swithin is connected with any heavy rains that fall from July 15th into August. Naturally, the farmers will welcome the rain for the crops. However, summer visitors, here for just a short time, will hope for sun and hot weather.

Early August brings the first delicious crop of corn. One of the newer types of corn is "peaches and cream" corn, a combination of bright yellow kernels and white ones mixed in to make a delicious sweet corn enjoyed on or off the cob.

The secret to Perfect Corn on the Cob is in the length of time that it is boiled.

Perfect Corn on the Cob

6 cobs corn

Butter, salt and pepper

Husk the corn, clearing every strand of silk. Trim off the stem and the top of the corn. Bring water to a boil. (Do not add salt or sugar as your mother often did.) Add corn to the water and cook uncovered 7–9 minutes. Drain the corn as soon as tender. Roll the corn in butter and salt and pepper to taste.

Many nights, when the first crop of corn comes in, we will make a meal of nothing but corn. It may not be a nutritionally sound meal but it certainly is one that I love! An easy way to do corn is on the barbeque.

Barbequed Corn

Soak unhusked corn in cold water about 1 hour. Peel back husks and remove the silk. Pull the husks back up to cover the ear and place on the grill of the barbeque, turning occasionally until done (about 20 minutes). Remove the husk. Roll in butter and salt and pepper to taste.

THERE ARE A NUMBER of ways to enjoy corn. One of my favourites is Corn Fritters. The first time that I ever tried a corn fritter was at a restaurant in Macon, Georgia. George and I were attending a conference in this southern U.S. state and we were eating in a small diner (with little in the way of elegant ambience) that served inexpensive but delicious meals. We both ordered our dinners and, as a side dish, the waitress brought a half dozen of the golden fritters and a jar of syrup. One bite and we were hooked! They are easy to make and I don't know of a single soul who doesn't love them.

Corn Fritters

1 cup fresh sweet corn (canned or frozen corn may be used
    out of season)
1/2 tsp salt
1/2 cup milk
2 eggs
2 cups flour
2 tsp baking powder

Mix all of the ingredients into a thick batter and drop by spoonfuls into hot fat 1/2 inch deep. Cook about 3 minutes on each side or until golden in colour. Drain on paper towel. Serve hot with butter and maple syrup.

Corn Chowder is another way to use corn and on a cool evening in late August it makes a nice appetizer.

Corn Chowder

1/2 cup salt pork, chopped

4 tbsp onion, chopped

1/4 cup celery, chopped

2 tbsp green pepper, chopped

1 cup raw potatoes, peeled and diced

1/2 tsp salt

2 cups water

2 tbsp flour

2 cups warm milk

2 cups corn kernels

Chopped parsley

Sauté salt pork in a large saucepan. Add onion, celery and green pepper and sauté. Add potatoes, salt and water and simmer until potatoes are done. Add flour, milk and corn.

Cook until all ingredients are heated thoroughly. Sprinkle with chopped parsley and serve hot. (This soup can also be a meal on its own. Serve with a salad and hot rolls and you have a quick supper.)

Serves 6

SUMMERTIME IN CANADA IS the time that families most enjoy our many parks with their majestic forests and pristine lakes and rivers. Camping is experiencing a renewed popularity particularly among families with young children. With any downturn in the economy, one of the first places that people generally cut back in their budget is in vacation spending. Camping provides a less expensive way of having a holiday and many of our parks provide outstanding facilities for campers of all ages.

My great-grandson Mickey and his Grade Six classmates went on a school camping trip to Algonquin Park. It started raining as they arrived at the park and continued to do so for three days. The children and their leaders put up tents in the rain, hiked in the rain, swam in the rain and slept in sleeping bags that were soaked by the rain. It was so wet that they ate peanut butter sandwiches morning, noon and night for three days. When they arrived home Mickey pronounced that it was "the best trip I was ever on!" The ridiculous thing is that he meant every word of it.

Cooking at a campsite can be challenging. It is not often possible to have items that need refrigeration so fresh fruits and vegetables and tinned or dried foods will often be a big part of the camper's food supply. Pork and Beans have been a staple of the camper's diet for years. This next recipe gives the dish a little bit of zip and takes it out of the "Oh no, not pork and beans again" ranking often given by children.

Pork and Beans

Piece of salt pork
2 15-oz cans pork and beans in tomato sauce
1 15-oz can kidney beans
1 pkg onion soup mix
1 cup tomato ketchup
1/2 cup water
2 tbsp prepared mustard (or 1 tbsp Dijon mustard)
2 tbsp brown sugar
2 tbsp cider vinegar

Precook the salt pork on your portable barbeque or over the campfire. Combine the pork and beans, kidney beans, onion soup, ketchup, water, mustard, sugar and vinegar in a 2-quart casserole (a cast iron pot is your best bet for campfire cooking). Bury the salt pork in the mixture. Cook over the campfire or on the portable barbeque until thoroughly heated.

Makes 6–8 servings

Campers often like to get out on the lake before the sun comes up and catch their dinner for that night. There's nothing that beats fresh-caught fish cooked over a fire!

Pan-Fried Bass

4 bass, cleaned, head and tails removed
Bacon drippings
Corn meal
Salt and pepper

Wipe the fish with a cloth dipped in lightly salted water. Rub the fish lightly with bacon drippings and roll in corn meal. Dust a little salt and pepper in the cavities. Heat bacon drippings in a cast iron fry pan. Drippings should be 1/4–1/2-inch deep and hot enough to brown a 1-inch cube of bread in 2 minutes (no hotter). Cook fish until it is browned on one side, about 4 minutes, then turn and brown on the other side. Drain on paper towel before serving.

Pan-fried potatoes and onions will make this a perfect outdoor dinner to enjoy under the early evening stars.

AUGUST USUALLY FINDS US in a daily routine of healthy outdoor activities, which most often means that people have developed healthy appetites to match. Isn't it lucky that this coincides with this time of bountiful harvest. The fruits and vegetables are ripening even faster than we are able to use them. Luckily, our forebears developed many ways to preserve our food—drying, smoking, salting, pickling, canning and freezing—and all of these methods are put to good use now.

When I was young and newly married I was very anxious to prove that I was an able (and frugal) cook. I decided that I would take some of the tomatoes, peppers, onions and cabbage that were so plentiful in our garden and make a piccalilli relish. I worked all day chopping and cooking the vegetables, sterilizing the jars and making what I hoped would be a delicious relish to use all the winter long. Unhappily, in my zeal I misread the recipe and instead of "1/4 cup salt" I added four cups of salt. (The fact that this didn't seem wrong to me gives evidence to the fact that the kitchen and cooking were rather new to me when I first married.) I served the relish at dinner that evening and George, to his credit, really tried to eat some but when his mouth puckered and tears came to his eyes I knew I had erred. Thankfully, my cooking did improve.

My son-in-law John enjoys peaches and his favourite way to "preserve" this fruit is in a pie—a method that usually preserves the peaches until about 10 minutes after the pie has cooled and his fork has attacked. My daughter Mary gave me her recipe for John's favourite peach pie—Sour Cream Peach Pie.

Sour Cream Peach Pie

Pastry for a 9-inch pie shell
1/3 cup all-purpose flour
1/2 cup granulated sugar
1 cup thick dairy sour cream

5 cups peeled and quartered peaches
1/4 cup lightly packed brown sugar

Preheat oven to 450°F. Line a 9-inch pie plate with the pastry. Flute the edges but do not prick the pastry. With a rotary beater, beat flour, granulated sugar and sour cream until smooth. Arrange flat edge of the peach quarters on the pastry in concentric circles. Pour the sour cream mixture over the top. Bake for 15 minutes, then lower heat to 350°F and bake 25–30 minutes or until the filling is set. Sprinkle brown sugar over the hot pie and broil until sugar is melted. Serve warm.

Serves 6 (or 3 if you're sharing with my son-in-law John)

ANOTHER PIE THAT IS one of my favourites at this time of year is Concord Grape Pie. The Concord grape originated in Concord, Massachusetts, way back in 1836. Ephraim Wales Bull of Boston bought a home near Hawthorne's "Wayside Inn" and set about breeding a good sturdy grapevine that could endure the rigours of the New England climate. He found a small vine on his property that bore grapes of excellent flavour and he spent the next six years cultivating the vine. The fame of his vines became known throughout the land and nurserymen came to him for slips with which to start their own vineyards. Soon the Concord grape became the most famous and sought after in the country.

Here, then, is the recipe for Concord Grape Pie (with special thanks to Ephraim Wales Bull).

Concord Grape Pie

Concord grapes
4 tbsp flour
1 1/4 cups sugar
Pastry for one 9-inch pie crust (plus extra for the lattice
*   work topping)*
2 tbsp butter

Wash enough grapes (free of stems) to fill a 9-inch pie tin and make a rounded mound. Squeeze pulp from grapes into a saucepan, reserving skins. Bring pulp to a boil. Strain out the seeds, and mix pulp and skins. Stir in 2 tbsp flour and 1 cup sugar. Line pie plate with pastry. Combine 1/4 cup sugar and 2 tbsp flour. Sprinkle on the bottom of the crust. Add grape filling. Add butter in the centre of the grape mixture. Cover the pie with a lattice topping. Bake in a 450°F oven for 10 minutes. Reduce heat to 400°F for 10 minutes, then bake for 30 minutes at 350°F.

Serves 6–8

If Concord grapes are favourites of yours you may want to try this recipe for Concord Grape Jelly that can be preserved and enjoyed all winter long.

Concord Grape Jelly

Wash underripe grapes and remove stems. Place in kettle
with 1/2 cup water for each 4 cupfuls of grapes. Boil the
grapes until soft, then strain through cheesecloth or a jelly
bag. Measure juice. Boil for 5 minutes. Add 1 cup of sugar for
each cup of juice. Continue boiling until jelly "sheets" from the
spoon (220°F). Pour at once into sterilized glasses. Seal with
paraffin.

Blue to the north is a sky so clear
It means the corner of the year
Has been turned, from now on all
Leaves and men face to the Fall.

—*R.P.T. Coffin*

All dressed up for the first day at school.

September

The first weekend in September is the Labour Day holiday, the last long weekend of the summer and the day before the children return to the classroom for the start of another school year.

Whenever I think of the first day of school I am reminded of a good friend, Dr. Ed Wilk, and the story of his son's start to kindergarten. The bus arrived at the end of the driveway on schedule and Ed helped his young son up the steps and onto the bus. He was quite unprepared for what happened next. A back window of the bus opened and Ed's son scrambled out of the bus, tears streaming down his face. Ed drove him to school. Every day for the next week Ed had to follow the bus on its route, waving continuously to his young son whose face was pressed to the rear window of the bus. Finally, after more than a week of this ritual, Ed's son announced that he could go to school on the bus by himself and daddy didn't need to follow him anymore. I truly admired Ed's patience!

Pray as though no work would help, and work as though no prayer would help.

—German proverb

FOR MANY, THE LABOUR Day holiday is the weekend to close up the cottage for the winter. Meals on this weekend are usually very interesting as all of the leftovers, both fresh and frozen, are emptied from the refrigerator. Finally, the boat has been put away, the water-pipes emptied, the door locked and another cottage season has ended.

It's tempting, when shopping at this time of year, to buy so many fresh fruits and vegetables that when you get home you wonder how on earth to use them all before they spoil. When the produce looks so good, it's hard to resist; happily, there are many mouthwatering ways to use it.

Deep Dish Pear Pie

6 cups pears, sliced
3 tbsp lemon juice
1/2 cup sugar
2 tbsp flour
1/2 tsp cinnamon
1/4 tsp nutmeg
Butter
Pastry crust

Sprinkle pears with lemon juice. Sift sugar, flour, cinnamon and nutmeg. Mix with pears. Place mixture in buttered ovenproof dish. Dot with butter. Cover pie with pastry crust. Bake in a hot oven (425°F) for 30 minutes or until pears are tender.

Stewed Cherries

4 cups cherries

1 1/2 cups boiling water

1 cup sugar

Remove stems and pits from cherries. Drop into boiling water. When tender, add sugar and cook 2 minutes longer.

Serves 4

This next recipe needs to be used early in September when it's still possible to find green tomatoes on the vines or at the markets.

Green Tomato Mincemeat

Boiling water

3 lb green tomatoes, chopped

3 lb apples, peeled and chopped

2 1/2 cups seeded raisins

1 cup chopped suet

8 cups brown sugar

2 tsp salt

1 cup cider vinegar

1 tbsp cinnamon
1 tsp nutmeg
1 tsp ground cloves
Juice and grated rind of 1 orange

In a large saucepan, pour the boiling water over the tomatoes. Drain. Repeat the process. Place the tomatoes in a large covered pot. Add the apples, raisins, suet, brown sugar and salt; cook over medium heat for 30 minutes. Add the vinegar, cinnamon, nutmeg, cloves and the orange juice and rind. Simmer slowly, stirring occasionally, until the mixture is thick, about 2 hours. When done, the mincemeat is ready for use as a filling for tarts and pies. Extra mincemeat can be stored by immediately pouring it into hot, sterilized pint canning jars. Seal and process the jars in a boiling water bath or steam canner for 25 minutes.

Makes about 12 pints

This recipe for Sweet and Sour Pepper Jam is a wonderful way to use your extra red peppers. The jam/relish is good on hamburgers and, when mixed with cream cheese, makes an excellent spread for crackers. It may also be used to glaze a rack of spareribs.

Sweet and Sour Pepper Jam

12 large red peppers
1 tbsp salt
2 cups sugar
2 cups vinegar

Put the peppers through the fine disk of a food mill or mince finely in a food processor. Sprinkle the peppers with salt and let stand 3 hours. Pour the pulp into a fine sieve and run cold water through it to remove some of the salt. Put the pulp into a saucepan; add sugar and vinegar and bring to a boil, stirring constantly until you are sure all the sugar is dissolved. Reduce heat and simmer until the jam gets quite thick. Pour into hot, sterilized jars and seal.

Yields 2 1/2 pints

Edna's Rose Potpourri

At the end of summer the last of the roses are in bloom. Roses make a delightful potpourri. Gather the petals after the dew has died. Spread the petals on an old cotton sheet that has been laid in a cool, dark place such as a storage cupboard or an attic room, and allow the petals to dry for 4–5 days. Put the dried petals in a bowl alternating layers of petals with layers of salt. Mix in crushed orris root, if you have it, and then add scents that appeal to you. Cedar chips, lavender, orange peel, rosemary, geranium leaves or verbena are all ingredients that will mix well with the dried rose petals to freshen any room.

SATURDAY MORNINGS WILL USUALLY find us at the Farmers' Market in town. Farmers' markets are terrific places to buy the freshest of the area's fruits and vegetables. Usually what you buy was picked just hours before in the nearby fields. Today we picked up some peaches, pears, apples and grapes as well as cucumbers, cabbage and peppers. Some of what we bought will be eaten fresh, but we will use the extra produce to can, pickle or freeze, to enjoy all through the winter.

Cucumber Relish has a fresh, crisp taste that sets it apart from other relishes.

Cucumber Relish

24 cups cucumbers, ends removed, but not peeled

4 cups medium onions

1 cup salt

9 cups cold water

6 cups sugar

5 cups vinegar

1/2 tsp turmeric

1 tsp mustard seed

1 tsp celery seed

Put cucumbers and onions through the medium blade of a food mill. Mix with the salt in a bowl and cover with the water. Let stand 3 hours. Drain. Boil the sugar and vinegar to make a syrup. Add the vegetables and spices and simmer until the vegetables are tender. Ladle into hot, sterilized jars and seal.

Yields about 7 pints

When making relish, it is wise to remember that onions and hot peppers contain juices that sting and burn. Handle them as little as possible. Be especially careful if you have any scratches on your hands. Use a wooden spoon to push the onions and peppers through the food mill. Do not touch your eyes or any tender skin area while working with onions and hot peppers. Wash your hands carefully when you have finished. Remember that a dose of hot pepper juice can make your hands burn for as long as 12 hours.

Now that I have warned you, here is a delicious relish recipe that will add zip to anything that you choose to serve with it.

India Relish

8 or 10 green tomatoes
4 large onions
6 large green peppers
1/4 cup salt

3 tbsp dry mustard

2 tbsp ground ginger

3/4 cup sugar

1/2 tsp ground cloves

1/2 tsp ground allspice

2 tbsp celery seed

4 cups vinegar

Put the vegetables through the fine blade of a food mill. Combine the remaining ingredients in a large saucepan and simmer and stir until sugar and salt are dissolved. Add the chopped vegetables to the syrup and bring to a boil. Boil slowly for 30 minutes, stirring frequently. Ladle into hot, sterilized jars and seal.

Yields about 6 pints

Pepper Relish

12 sweet red peppers

12 green peppers

12 medium onions

2 cups vinegar

1 1/2 cups sugar

2 tbsp salt

1 tbsp celery seed

Put the peppers and onions through the medium blade of a food mill. Put the chopped vegetables in a large bowl and cover with boiling water. Let stand 5 minutes. Drain. Combine the vinegar, sugar and seasonings in a saucepan and boil for 5 minutes. Add the vegetables and boil for 10 minutes. Pack in hot, sterilized jars and seal.

Yields about 4 1/2 pints

NO COOKBOOK WOULD BE complete without a recipe for Chili Sauce. Our family has many recipes for this loved sauce but I think that my favourite is from Mother McCann. Many September Saturdays would find us in her large kitchen working over the wood stove turning quart after quart baskets of tomatoes, onions and peppers into dozens and dozens of jars of Chili Sauce. Heaven help us if we should run out of sauce before the next year's crop of tomatoes was ripe!

Mother McCann's Chili Sauce

24 large ripe tomatoes
4 large onions
8 green peppers
4 tbsp salt
1 cup sugar
1 tbsp cinnamon

1 tbsp ground cloves

1 tbsp allspice

1 tbsp dry mustard

5 cups vinegar

Put tomatoes, onions and peppers through the coarse blade of a food mill. Cook slowly with the salt, sugar, spices and vinegar until thick (about 45–60 minutes). Stir occasionally. Ladle into hot, sterilized jars and seal.

Yields about 8 pints

SEPTEMBER IS A MARVELLOUS time to enjoy the brilliant fall colours. A country drive for even a few hours can leave you almost breathless from the beauty of the scarlet, yellow and orange leaves set against a brilliant blue sky.

Several years ago, my friend Emily joined me in September on a drive through southern and central Ontario. We stayed at a number of tiny inns and bed and breakfast places in small towns in the region. The fall scenery was spectacular and at the end of each day's drive we were treated to some of the finest cuisine offered in Ontario. I was proud to be able to show Emily some of our province's excellent restaurants.

Emily is, herself, a marvellous cook and she has shared with me a few of her most treasured recipes. I am happy to be able to share these with you. French Garlic Soup is a delicious and different soup that Emily serves frequently at dinner parties.

French Garlic Soup

24 cloves garlic, peeled but not cut

2 tbsp oil or drippings

8 cups boiling water or stock

Pinch each nutmeg, tarragon and ground cloves

Salt and pepper to taste

4 egg yolks

6 slices French bread, toasted

In a large heavy soup pot, lightly sauté garlic cloves in oil until they are golden. Add boiling water or stock and seasonings and simmer slowly for about 20 minutes. Allow to cool slightly, then process in a blender or through a food mill. Return to soup pot, heat slightly and add egg yolks gradually, stirring continuously. Do not allow soup to boil. Serve immediately, poured over toasted French bread.

Serves 6

Our American friends often eat popovers (what we call Yorkshire pudding) as we would eat rolls, so they may be eaten with almost any entrée. I especially enjoy them with a roast beef dinner. This is an easy recipe for Popovers that melt in your mouth.

Popovers

2 tbsp water
1 cup milk
1 cup sifted flour
1/2 tsp salt
2 eggs, beaten

Mix ingredients together. Grease muffin tins thoroughly. Half fill the muffin cups with batter. Place in a cold oven. Set the oven at 400°F. Leave for 30 minutes. Turn off the heat. If the popovers are not brown enough leave them in the oven another 10 minutes.

Makes 1 dozen

Emily presently lives in Philadelphia but she enjoys spending time on the east coast both in the United States and in Canada. She has developed a love for shellfish and often uses recipes that call for a variety of seafood. This recipe for Thin Noodles with Shellfish is delicious and elegant enough to serve to company.

Thin Noodles with Shellfish

1 tbsp olive oil

1 carrot, finely diced

1 medium onion, finely diced

3/4–1 lb lobster, shelled and cut into large pieces

1 lb pink shrimp, shelled

1 tbsp tomato paste

1 cup water

1 clove garlic, crushed, in 3 tbsp oil

Pinch powdered saffron

Salt and freshly ground black pepper

12 oz thin spaghetti or vermicelli, preferably bought fresh
*   from a specialty shop*

Lightly coat the carrot and onion in the olive oil, then add
lobster, shrimp, tomato paste diluted in the 1 cup water, garlic and saffron. Mix well and season with salt and pepper.
Cook, covered, 8–10 minutes. Meanwhile poach the spaghetti
in simmering water: 2 minutes if the pasta is fresh or 7–8
minutes if the pasta is dried. The pasta must be tender but still
chewy. To serve, fold the sauce into the spaghetti and serve hot
in a deep vegetable dish.

Serves 4

See what a riot of colour!
Hark, what a riot of sound!
Golden grain and golden leaves
Rustling on the ground.

Here is a wealth worth hoarding,
Here is the gold of God!
The sun upon the harvest fields,
And the gleam of goldenrod.

—*Marion Doyle*

THIS IS ALSO THE time of year when the baseball season is winding down and the playoffs are on the horizon. I readily admit to being a "dyed in the wool" Blue Jays fan. I follow our boys' games on radio and television and several times a season I am lucky enough to see a game live at the beautiful SkyDome. My growing love of baseball has been a surprise to my friends, and even to me. I used to tell my husband George that watching a baseball game was akin to watching grass grow. Then in 1985 my friend Jake Frampton took me to a game between the Jays and the New York Yankees. At the time the Jays held a very slim lead over the second-place Yankees. The Jays played a spectacular game. Before long I was wildly applauding each and every play and a blasé spectator had become an avid fan.

It's fun to have friends over to watch the games on television and I like to serve my own version of "crackerjacks." To do this I need to make a Popcorn Syrup to pour over the popcorn.

Popcorn Syrup for Caramel Nut Popcorn

1/2 cup sugar
1/2 cup dark corn syrup
1/2 tsp salt

Combine sugar and corn syrup with salt. When popcorn is popped, reduce the heat to medium and pour the popcorn syrup over the popcorn. Mix in 1 cup of salted peanuts. Stir for 2 or 3 minutes to coat the popcorn and the peanuts well, then turn out onto a large sheet of foil. Spread evenly and let stand to allow the syrup to harden a bit. Let cool thoroughly and serve, in bowls, to your fellow fans.

Going for a walk with the family pet.

October

E arly October finds the leaf colour at its spectacular best. Helen B. Henderson wrote a poem, "Autumn Glory," that describes so well the beauty of this month.

> *The trees their flaming torches raise*
> *Above the sun-kissed land;*
> *The sumacs in these autumn days*
> *In crimson velvet stand.*
> *And soft in autumn's mellow light*
> *All nature seems to rest,*
> *While in the lakes' calm mirror bright*
> *Trees view the radiant dress.*
> *Oh! glad the glamour of the spring*
> *And gay the summer time;*
> *But autumn days! No season brings*
> *A beauty such as thine.*
> *So in the face of ripened age*
> *May light and love appear,*
> *As when the brilliant autumn days*
> *Crown bright the closing year.*

IT'S PLEASANT TO GO for a drive to enjoy the scenery but as well it's nice to have a destination in mind. Why not choose one of the many fall fairs that are so popular on weekends in September and October? The fairs offer something for everyone in the family; pet shows, equestrian events, sheep-shearing and cow-milking demonstrations, arts and crafts displays and produce competitions are just a few of the events to enjoy. Last year our seniors' group entered a number of "goodies" in the baking competition. Muffins, brownies and chocolate chip cookies were first-place winners and our tea biscuits were the "Baked Goods Grand Champions." We were a mighty proud group as we watched the chairman "ribbon" our efforts.

Probably the most popular area at the fair—in our family at least—is the barn where the community supper is served. The ladies of the community spend hours putting together a meal that includes some of the tastiest produce available. Roast chicken, mashed potatoes, cauliflower, turnips all served piping hot—just remembering makes my mouth water.

Desserts are also very popular at these dinners. The next two recipes come to you courtesy of the hardworking ladies' group in our area, which provides the meal at our local fair.

Peach Candy Pie

4 cups peeled, sliced fresh peaches

3/4 cup sugar

2 tbsp instant tapioca

1/2 cup sifted flour

1/4 cup light brown sugar, firmly packed

4 tbsp softened butter or margarine

Unbaked 9-inch pie shell

Combine peaches, sugar and tapioca. Set aside. Combine the flour and brown sugar, then rub in the butter until the mixture resembles coarse crumbs. Sprinkle 1/3 of the brown sugar mixture over the bottom of the pie shell. Pour in the peach mixture and cover with the remaining brown sugar mixture. Bake in a preheated 450°F oven for 10 minutes. Reduce heat to 350°F and bake about 25 minutes longer or until peaches are tender and the top is golden. Cool well before serving.

Crunchy Apple Pie

Unbaked 9-inch pie shell

5 1/2 cups peeled, cored and sliced cooking apples

1/2 cup granulated sugar

1/4 cup brown sugar, firmly packed

3 tbsp flour

1/4 tsp salt

1/2 tsp cinnamon

1/4 tsp nutmeg

Preheat oven to 375°F. Combine above ingredients, mix well and spoon into pie shell.

Topping:
3/4 cup flour
1/4 cup sugar
1/4 cup brown sugar, firmly packed
1/3 cup butter, softened

Mix all 4 ingredients with a fork or pastry blender until crumbly. Sprinkle mixture evenly over the apples. Bake for 40–50 minutes until apples are soft and topping is golden. Cool on wire rack. This is particularly good when served warm with fresh cream.

FROM THE TIME THAT the first settlers arrived in Canada, early October, after the harvest, has been the time when families paused to give thanks for all good things given to us. Although each family celebrates in its own way, generally speaking this is the most family-oriented holiday next to Christmas. Family is one of the most important parts of our lives. If we are grateful for something good in our lives, that something very often is our family.

We McCanns are no exception. Although we are widely scattered, nearly all of our family members make a great effort to attend the family get-together. We serve our Thanksgiving meal on Sunday following the morning church service. Roast stuffed turkey is our favourite and as our family has grown in numbers so has the size of our turkey.

Today, getting the turkey ready is as simple as removing the plastic wrap covering, taking out the nicely packaged giblets and placing the bird in the oven. For those of you who consider this a "chore" I offer these instructions taken from one of my old cookbooks: "Select a young turkey: remove all of the feathers carefully, singe it over a burning newspaper on the top of the stove; then 'draw' it nicely, being very careful not to break any of the internal organs. Remove the crop carefully; cut off the neck close to the body. Rinse out the inside of the turkey several times and in the next to last rinse mix a teaspoonful of baking soda. Rinse again, then wipe the turkey dry, inside and out, with a clean cloth. Rub the inside with some salt, then stuff the breast and body with 'Dressing for Fowls.'" Thanksgiving is a much easier holiday than it used to be!

Bread stuffing can add a special flavour to the roasting bird. This Bread Stuffing with Sage recipe is one that has been in our family for generations.

Bread Stuffing with Sage

4 cups dry bread crumbs
1/2 cup melted butter
1 egg, beaten
1/2 tsp salt
1/4 tsp pepper
1 tsp brown sugar
1 tbsp minced onion
1 tsp dried ground sage

Mix bread crumbs and melted butter together. Add beaten egg, seasonings, sugar, onion and sage. When all ingredients have been well mixed, decide if a more moist dressing is desired. If so, add some hot liquid—this can be stock or water.

Makes 4 cups

If children are a part of your Thanksgiving dinner crowd it's probably wise to keep your choice of vegetables to the "known and loved." Carrots are almost always a kid's favourite and with just a minor addition they can be made special for the adults in your family.

Company Carrots

1 1/2 1-lb bags carrots
1 1/2 tbsp butter or margarine
1/2 tsp salt
1/4 tsp sugar
1 tbsp chopped chives or parsley

Cut carrots into matchstick-thin strips. In a 3-quart saucepan over high heat in about 2 inches of water, heat carrots to boiling. Reduce heat to low. Cover and simmer 2–3 minutes until carrots are tender-crisp. Drain the carrots and return them to the saucepan. Add the butter, salt and sugar and toss the carrots. Remove saucepan from the heat. Serve children's portions immediately. Stir in chives or parsley to remaining carrots and serve.

Serves 8

Green Beans with Almonds

1 lb green beans
1 1/2 tbsp butter or margarine
1 clove garlic, minced
1 4-oz pkg sliced almonds
1/2 tsp salt
1/8 tsp pepper

Place the beans in boiling, lightly salted water. Cook until tender-crisp. Drain. In a large skillet over medium-high heat stir butter and garlic until butter melts. Add almonds and brown lightly. Add beans, salt and pepper. Toss gently. Place in serving dish.

Makes 6 servings

I MUST CONFESS THAT, although I love to cook, my attempts to make a delicious smooth gravy have never met with much success. My grandmother made good gravy, my mother made good gravy and my sister makes good gravy. I began to suspect that perhaps I had inherited some unknown genetic defect that prevented me from making good gravy. It was not until I followed the instructions given to me by my grandson Marshall's wife, Jamie, that my gravy left the congealed lumps behind and became, not only edible, but downright delicious. Here, for those of you who need help as much as I did, is Jamie's recipe.

Jamie's Lump-Free Gravy

While turkey is roasting, prepare giblets and neck to use in the gravy. Place gizzard, heart and neck in a 3-quart saucepan, add water to cover and heat to boiling. Reduce heat to low; cover and simmer 45 minutes. Add the liver and simmer about 15 minutes more or until giblets are tender. Drain, reserving the liquid. Pull the meat from the neck and chop coarsely with the giblets. Cover and refrigerate the meat and broth separately.

When the turkey is done, place on a large warm platter; keep warm. Remove rack from the roasting pan. Pour pan drippings into a medium bowl and set the pan aside. Let the drippings stand a few seconds until fat separates from the meat juice. Return 3 tbsp of fat from the drippings to the roasting pan; skim off and discard any remaining fat. Add giblet broth to meat juice in the bowl to make 2 1/2 cups. Place roasting pan over low heat on stovetop element. Into the fat in the roasting pan stir flour (approx. 2–3 tbsp) until blended; gradually stir in meat-juice–broth mixture and 1 chicken bouillon cube and cook, stirring until gravy boils and thickens slightly and the brown bits are loosened from the bottom of the pan. Add chopped giblets and neck meat and heat through. Pour gravy into a heated gravy boat and serve.

No turkey dinner would be complete without cranberries. Often we have cranberry sauce or jelly with the meat. However, my sister Sarah gave me this terrific recipe for Cranberry–Apple Salad, which is a different way to enjoy the berries.

Cranberry–Apple Salad

1 medium thin-skinned orange, cut into eighths (seeds removed)

1 medium apple, cored and cut into eighths

2 cups fresh or frozen cranberries

1 1/4 cups sugar

1 small pkg orange or lemon Jell-O

1 envelope unflavoured gelatin

1 cup cold water

Grated peel and juice of 1 lemon

Force orange, apple and cranberries through fine blades of a food chopper or whirl in a food processor until chopped fine. Add sugar, mix well. Chill, stirring occasionally to dissolve sugar, for 2 hours or overnight. Prepare orange or lemon Jell-O according to the package directions. In a small saucepan soften the unflavoured gelatin in 1 cup cold water. Cook over low heat, stirring until dissolved. Add to Jell-O along with lemon peel and juice. Chill until it is the consistency of un-beaten egg whites. Fold in cranberry–apple–orange mixture until thoroughly blended. Pour into a 6-cup ring mould. Chill until firm. Unmould onto a serving plate. Garnish with Frosted Cranberries.

Frosted Cranberries

In a small bowl lightly beat 1 egg white. Dip 1 cup cranberries in egg, roll each cranberry in granulated sugar to coat. Let dry at least 30 minutes.

AS WE NEAR THE end of October, the days and nights become dramatically cooler, giving us a hint of the winter that will be coming all too soon. During this harvest month I remember back to our days in a rural parish on Canada's east coast. In those days the farmers and their families would band together to become one large crew, moving from farm to farm and working together to gather the crops.

For old-time dinners the women were quite ingenious in designing ways to keep things hot during the long trips from the farm kitchens to the cloth-covered tables in the yard of the property where the harvesting was taking place on that particular day. One clever lady made what she called a "hay cooker." In a wooden box with a tight cover, she packed loose hay; she then set her covered dish in a hollow in the hay, covered it with more hay, then fastened the lid of the box tightly. The food stayed nice and hot until serving time. Another similar method of keeping the food hot was to use something called a "freestone." Soapstones heated to the right temperature on the kitchen stove were placed in a small metal tub. Pots of food set on the stones stayed hot for hours. One of the most popular meals at harvesting was beef stew. This recipe, Absent Cook's Stew, was a particular favourite because there was no need to watch this stew as it cooked.

Absent Cook's Stew

2 lb stewing beef, cubed

3 medium carrots, peeled and sliced

2 medium onions, peeled and sliced

3 medium potatoes, peeled and quartered

1 small yellow turnip, peeled and cubed

1 (10 1/2 oz) can condensed tomato soup

1/2 soup can water

2 tbsp vinegar

1 tsp salt

Pinch of pepper

1 bay leaf

You will need a heavy casserole with a tight-fitting lid. Place the meat cubes in the casserole and arrange the vegetables around and through the cubes. Combine the remaining ingredients and pour over meat and vegetables. Cover and bake in a 275°F oven for about 5 hours. The meat will be brown and delicious and the gravy will have a rich flavour.

Serves 4–6

T H E   E N D   O F   T H I S month of harvest brings us to
Halloween. How much I enjoy this night! Watching the little
"ghosts and goblins" as they stagger under the load of their
treat bags brings memories of my own children on this night.
Although I could never claim to be an accomplished seam-
stress, I loved to make costumes for the girls to wear on
Halloween. One year I decided to make Julia into a little yellow canary. I bought several feather dusters and hand sewed
each and every feather on her little wings and tail. It was an
enormously time-consuming job but the look on Julia's little
face when she saw the finished costume was well worth all
the effort.

The treat that my girls loved most was a caramel apple.
Over the years I think I've made more than a thousand but
each succeeding generation of children seems to love them as
much as ever.

Caramel Apples

3 cups pure maple syrup
1 cup light sweet cream
4 tbsp butter
1–1 1/2 cups non-instant milk powder
10–12 apples with sticks

Mix the maple syrup and cream in a large saucepan. Slowly
bring the mixture to a simmer, stirring constantly. If the mixture begins to curdle, it is heating too rapidly. Immediately reduce the heat and continue cooking. The mixture will not be

harmed. When it simmers, continue cooking the mixture to the soft ball stage (mixture makes a soft ball when tested in cold water), stirring often. Pour the hot sauce into a large mixing bowl. Add the butter. Cool slightly. Beat in the milk powder until the still warm mixture will pour very slowly.

Have a pot of boiling water ready. If the caramel mixture hardens or cools too much, set the mixing bowl over boiling water for a minute or two until the caramel softens again. Coat each apple by turning it in the warm caramel sauce. Let the excess drip off. Place the coated apples on a buttered cookie sheet in the refrigerator until the caramel hardens.

From ghoulies and ghosties and long-leggety beasties
And things that go bump in the night,
Good Lord, deliver us!

—Anonymous

Another Halloween favourite in our house is Scotch Toffee. My great-grandmother often made this candy for us and its simplicity makes for an easy but delicious treat.

Scotch Toffee

3/4 cup fresh butter
2 lb yellow sugar
Enough cream to make thin batter

Melt the butter slowly and when fully melted add the sugar. Remove from heat, mix thoroughly and stir in sufficient cream to make the mixture the consistency of a thin batter. Now place on the stove and stir until the boiling point is reached. After this it must *not* be stirred at all. Boil very slowly until it feels tough, but not brittle, when tested by cooling a little in cold water. Now pour onto buttered shallow trays and cool slowly. Cut into squares. The success of this recipe depends largely on slow boiling and cooling.

Edna's Kitchen Hints

- Add two or three egg shells to your soup stock and simmer ten minutes. The shells will help clarify the broth.

- Combine all ingredients for an oil and vinegar dressing in a screw-top jar. Add an ice cube and shake well. Remove and discard the ice cube and the dressing will be extra smooth and well mixed.

- A clean coffee percolator is perfect for cooking asparagus. The asparagus stands upright and the tops steam perfectly while the stems become tender in the boiling water.

- To absorb cabbage odour while cooking, place a small cup of vinegar on the range or add a wedge of lemon to the cooking pot.

- Before storing carrots, remove the tops, as they drain the moisture from the carrots, leaving them limp and dry.

- Never immerse mushrooms in water when cleaning. They will absorb too much liquid.

- For the best french fries, first let the cut potatoes stand in cold water for an hour before frying. Dry thoroughly before cooking. The trick then is to fry them twice. The first time just fry them for a few minutes and blot off the grease. Then fry until golden brown. They're delicious.

- To freshen vegetables that are wilted or blemished, pick off the brown edges and soak the vegetables for an hour in cold water to which the juice of a lemon or a few tablespoons of vinegar has been added.

- To remove corn silk from corn on the cob dampen a toothbrush and brush downward on the corn cob. Every strand should come off.

- Cottage cheese will remain fresh longer if you store it upside down in your refrigerator.

- To prevent cheese from becoming mouldy store it in a tightly covered container with some sugar cubes.

- Keep bacon slices from sticking together by rolling the package into a tube shape and securing with a rubber band before you refrigerate.

- When cooking a roast, instead of using a metal roasting rack, make a grid of carrots and celery and place the meat or poultry on it. The vegetables add a nice flavour to the pan drippings.

- If you cry when you chop onions, try putting the onions in the refrigerator to chill them before peeling. Cold onions are much less likely to cause tears.

Looking forward to an outing.

November

No warmth nor cheer nor ease,
No comfortable feel in any member,
No shade, no shine, no butterflies, no bees
No fruits, no flowers, no leaves, no birds
No—vember.

This is the way Englishman Thomas Hood saw November and many of us, I think, feel the same way about this grey and dreary month. November 1st does give us a reason to rejoice. This is All Saints' Day, a day when we pause to remember and give thanks for all those good people who make our lives a little better. George used to say that a saint is an ordinary believer in God, who, on his or her journey through life, has shared faith by being concerned about others. This is a good day to think of those "saints" who have touched our lives—a patient school teacher, a doctor who has cured a sick child, a friend who shares our joys and our sorrows. These are people who touch our lives and give it meaning and worth.

Remembrance Day, November 11th, as if to commemorate the hurt and suffering, devastation and death of two world wars, is most often wet, dreary and cold. There is one light that glimmers in the darkness of Remembrance Day and that is the courage and self-sacrifice of men and women who died believing that they were stemming the spread of evil and preserving the best elements of our way of life. I hope that we never let that light go out. It is a worthy remembrance.

I often find myself doing a little more cooking in the month of November. The comfort of hot food and the familiar warmth of the kitchen are sure to lighten the dark days of November.

Cauliflower Soup is one of my favourite "comfort foods." This delicate creamy soup is delicious with sandwiches for lunch or served as a first course with dinner.

Cauliflower Soup

1 medium cauliflower

1 stalk celery, washed and cut into 1-inch pieces

1 thick slice lemon

2 tbsp butter

1 medium onion, peeled and diced

2 tbsp flour

1 cup of the water in which the cauliflower is cooked

3 cups chicken stock from which all fat has been removed

2 tsp salt

1/4 tsp pepper

1 cup light cream

Cook the cauliflower, celery pieces and slice of lemon in boiling water. When tender, drain and reserve the celery pieces and 1 cup of the water. Discard the lemon. Break the cauliflower into florets and reserve 1/2 cup of the tiniest for garnish. Melt the butter in a large pot and, when foaming, add the onion. Stir and cook until transparent. Add the flour, cook and stir until well blended. Slowly add the cup of cauliflower water, celery pieces and cauliflower florets, stirring constantly, until well blended. Add the stock, salt and pepper. Put this mixture through a food mill or blender and blend until smooth. Return the soup to the pot and simmer for 10–15 minutes. Add the light cream. Stir and bring to a boil. Just before serving, add the 1/2 cup florets. Serve from a heated tureen or in individual bowls.

Serves 4–6

I FIND THAT THE changeable November weather seems to wear down my resistance to illness. I will catch a cold or have a bout of 'flu more often in the month of November than in any other month.

Whatever the reason for the illness, I usually rely on the old and reliable "cure"—chicken soup. This recipe is quite filling and is almost a meal in itself. Although its medicinal qualities are unproven, my son-in-law Bruce claims that it has magical healing power. Try it yourself and see.

Cream of Chicken and Vegetable Soup

8 cups chicken stock from which all fat has been removed
1 tbsp potato flour
1/4 cup cold water

1 tbsp butter

1 cup carrots, peeled and finely diced

1 cup celery, washed and finely diced

1 cup onions, peeled and finely diced

3–4 cups cooked chicken, diced

1 cup peas, fresh or frozen

2 tsp salt

1 tsp pepper

2 egg yolks, lightly beaten

1/2 cup heavy cream

Bring the stock to a boil. Mix potato flour with the water, and, stirring, slowly pour into the stock and simmer. Melt the butter in a pan, add carrots, celery and onions. Sauté for 5–10 minutes or until onions are transparent, not brown. Add to stock. Add chicken meat and simmer for 15 minutes. Add peas, salt and pepper and simmer 5 minutes. Mix together the egg yolks and cream. Bit by bit add a small amount of the hot soup to the eggs and cream, stirring constantly. When a cup of the hot soup is blended with the egg mixture, pour it slowly into the soup, stirring continuously. Heat but do not boil. Serve from a heated tureen or in heated individual soup bowls.

Serves 6–8

The common cold, treated with decongestants, fluids and bed rest, will clear up in two weeks. Left completely alone, it should be gone in about fourteen days.

Whenever I do get sick, many of my mother's "tried, tested and true" remedies come to mind. Beef tea, mutton broth and arrowroot milk porridge are a few of Mother's popular "cures." However, the favourite, given to us when we had a cold (or the 'flu, or any other malaise) was Oatmeal Gruel. How I hated it! I think the curative power lay in the fact that you wanted to feel better just so that you wouldn't need another dose of the ghastly stuff. "Not feeling well? Perhaps a nice cup of gruel, pet..." was threat enough to make me feel better immediately. Perhaps you'd like to make up a pot of it as a preventive measure.

Oatmeal Gruel

Pour 4 tbsp of the best oatmeal, coarsely ground, into 2 cups of boiling water. Let it boil gently and stir it often until it becomes as thick as you wish. Then strain it, and add to the gruel while warm some butter, nutmeg and salt to taste. The sicker the patient the thinner should be the gruel.

Although modern medicine has given us a pill for almost everything, there are still those who believe in the curative powers of many foods. I have kept a list of various fruits and vegetables and the disease or illness that each may help. I thought that you might enjoy seeing these old-time "cure-alls."

Celery—for any form of rheumatism and nervous dys-
pepsia

Lettuce—for insomnia

Onions—for insomnia, coughs and colds, a complexion
curer

Carrots—for asthma

Eggs—beaten egg white, sugar and lemon juice will re-
lieve hoarseness

Cranberries—eaten raw are a fine tonic and will also cure
a headache

Sour oranges—highly recommended for rheumatism

Lemons—for feverish thirst, biliousness, low fevers,
rheumatism, colds, coughs and liver complaints

Bananas—for chronic diarrhea

Peanuts—for indigestion

NOVEMBER IS A GOOD month in which to do some
entertaining. George and I preferred to have close friends
over for dinner and an evening of cards or perhaps have a
very informal meal in front of the fire and just talk. It was
George's "time off" to relax and enjoy the company of friends.

As a senior I rarely have a large gathering but I still enjoy
having a small group for dinner and an evening of bridge. I
find that the table setting can make even the simplest dinner special. Flowers, candles, shiny silverware and glasses
and china that sparkle make an attractive and welcoming setting for your dinner. Here are some recipes that my friends
and I have enjoyed many times.

Luscious Shrimp Chowder

1 tbsp cooking oil
1 onion, chopped
1 clove garlic
1/2 can condensed tomato soup
2 1/2 cups boiling water
1/4 cup green peas
1/4 cup whole kernel corn
2 large potatoes, peeled and cubed
1 tsp salt
1/8 tsp chili powder
1/8 tsp marjoram
1/2 pkg (1 1/2 oz) cream cheese
2 cups milk
1/3 lb cleaned uncooked shrimp
2 eggs

Heat the oil in a deep saucepan. Add onion and garlic and cook until brown. Remove garlic. Add tomato soup, water, peas, corn, potatoes and seasonings and cook 20 minutes. Meanwhile soften cream cheese in a large bowl and gradually blend in milk. Stir the soup into the cheese and milk mixture. Return to the saucepan. (From this point on, soup must not boil.) Add shrimp, cook slowly for 10 minutes more. Beat eggs in a bowl. Gradually stir some of the soup into the eggs, then add egg–soup mixture to saucepan and cook chowder over low heat until heated through.

Makes 4 generous servings

Fillets of Sole Amandine

1/4 cup blanched almonds, coarsely chopped
3 tbsp softened butter or margarine
1/2 tsp salt
1/2 tsp paprika
1/8 tsp pepper
Grated peel of 1 lemon
1 lb frozen skinless fillets of sole, thawed

Combine almonds, butter, salt, paprika, pepper and lemon
peel in a small bowl and mix with a wooden spoon. Separate
thawed fish and cut into serving-size pieces. Arrange in a
baking dish and spread each piece with the almond butter.
Bake at 350°F (moderate) 15–20 minutes or until the fish
flakes easily when tested with a fork.

Makes 4 servings

Wild Rice

1 cup wild rice
2 cloves garlic, peeled and chopped
4 tbsp butter
1 tsp salt
8 Shiitake mushrooms

Bring 8 cups of water to a boil in a saucepan. Add rice, garlic, butter, salt and mushrooms. Lower heat to medium and cook for 40 minutes until the rice is soft. Just before serving, fish out the mushrooms, which should now be quite soft, and chop them very finely. Drain the remaining water from the rice, stir in the chopped mushrooms, add a little more butter and serve with the Fillets of Sole Amandine.

November's sky is chill and drear,
November's leaf is red and sear.

—Sir Walter Scott

Green Peas with Mint

Boil 2 cups green peas (fresh or frozen) until tender. Serve with 4 tbsp melted butter to which 2 tbsp chopped mint leaves have been added.

Herbed Crescent Rolls

1 8-oz pkg refrigerator crescent rolls
1/4 cup softened butter
1 tsp parsley flakes
1/2 tsp ground rosemary

Separate the crescent rolls and place on a greased cookie sheet. Combine the rest of the ingredients and spread evenly over the rolls. Roll up and bake as the package directs. Serve hot.

Makes 8 rolls

Peppermint Ice Cream

4 egg yolks

3/4 cup sugar

3 cups milk

1 cup heavy cream

1/2 tsp spirit of peppermint (usually available in drugstores)

4 oz peppermint candy, chopped

In a medium-size bowl, beat together egg yolks and sugar until pale yellow. Combine milk and cream in a saucepan and bring just to a simmer over low heat. Pour a little of this hot mixture into the egg yolks, stirring constantly, until mixture thickens slightly and coats the back of a spoon; do *not* boil. Cool to room temperature. Stir in spirit of peppermint. Pour mixture into container of a hand-cranked or electric ice cream freezer. Freeze following manufacturer's directions. When almost frozen, add peppermint candy and continue freezing until completely frozen.

If you are not lucky enough to have an ice cream freezer, you can do this recipe very simply. Buy a small container of French vanilla ice cream. Soften slightly and mix in chopped peppermint candy and the 1/2 tsp spirit of peppermint. Mix well. Refreeze and serve. Just light the candles and enjoy!

WE OFTEN SEE THE first snow of the season in this month. The children are ecstatic and the adults try to remember how to drive in the slippery white stuff. The commuters will grumble, but isn't it beautiful to see the snow-laden tree branches and children making snow angels on the front lawn? As children, my sister Sarah, my brother Ben and I would eagerly await the first snowfall. Our favourite snow was the heavy wet variety, which could be easily packed into snowballs or made into snowmen. It was my father who first suggested to us that snowmen were quite ordinary and that perhaps if we used our imagination we could make something more interesting. What a challenge!

We began by packing the snow into large balls and rolling them together. Next we carved away the snow that we didn't need. We used sticks and small rocks to complete our creation. When he came home my father declared that it was the finest snow dinosaur that he had ever seen. I still have the photograph in an old scrapbook and the smiles on our faces showed the pride we felt in our accomplishment.

Coming in from the cold, it's nice to warm up with a hot drink. Hot Spiced Milk is a drink that we enjoyed as children and when I have it now I am magically transported back to my childhood home.

Hot Spiced Milk

4 cups milk
1/2 cup evaporated milk, undiluted
1/2 tsp nutmeg
1/2 tsp ground cloves
3/4 tbsp sugar
1/8 tsp salt
Cinnamon sticks

Heat all the ingredients except the cinnamon sticks together in a large pot. Stir from time to time and do not allow to boil. When hot, pour into mugs and garnish each with an extra-long cinnamon-stick stirrer.

Makes 6 servings

Café au Lait is a favourite hot drink of many of my European friends and they tell me that the secret to good Café au Lait is in the pouring.

Café au Lait

Make 4 cups of coffee. Heat 4 cups of milk and pour it into a pitcher. With the pitcher in one hand and the coffeepot in the other, pour the milk and coffee simultaneously into each cup. Serve while frothy. Sugar may be added as desired.

Serves 5–6 with seconds

Here is one more hot drink to take away the November chill.

Hot Mocha Milk

1/4 cup instant coffee powder

1/3 cup quick chocolate-flavoured drink mix

1/4 cup sugar

5 cups very hot milk

In a heat-proof pitcher, blend coffee powder, chocolate drink mix and sugar. Add milk and stir until well combined.

Serves 5 generously

How welcome is the warm fireside, the steaming cup of chocolate, the comradeship of books and the love of family and friends!

Have you been naughty or nice?

December

December is a month of parties and celebrations, with Christmas and Hanukkah at the forefront. As the holiday season approaches I look forward to the rituals that are a big part of our family's life together. Lighting the advent candles, writing Christmas cards and decorating the house are just a few of the many things that we enjoy doing as a family. Pierre Berton has said, "To me, ritual is the glue that keeps society together. Family rituals, like vacations with the whole family, are very important things. To get a sense of community: that is what gives people peace of mind and security."

In the past few years our family has begun a new tradition for the festive season. Using the *Good Housekeeping* magazine, December issue, we replicate the prize-winning gingerbread houses that have been selected from entries from across North America. Several years ago I cut out the recipe for a "little country cottage" but I hadn't the courage to try to make it until my granddaughter Phyllis said that she would like to try it with me. Marg, Mary, Julia, Phyllis and I decided to follow the directions step by step and see if we could come close to the delightful result pictured in the magazine. It was less difficult than it appeared. As well, Phyllis and Julia, who have the patience of Job, were given the job of "finishing" the window frames, the front door wreath, the Christmas garlands and the other tiny details that the rest of us had neither the patience nor the perseverance to deal with. The result was a beautiful centrepiece for the Christmas table.

Now, each year, we get together to fashion this decorative table centrepiece and we look forward to this time spent together.

There is nothing that gives me more pleasure than to have our whole family together on a happy occasion. Christmas Day has always provided us with a chance to enjoy such a time. We gather first at the morning service of worship at our church before returning home to open the seemingly endless gaily wrapped packages handed out by our "elves," John and Bruce. Dinner is a delicious and noisy affair as each of us tries to catch up on days, weeks or months of news from relatives from afar.

For years our family enjoyed a goose for our Christmas dinner. Although turkey is the more popular bird these days, I still enjoy a goose and I particularly like it with chestnut stuffing. This recipe for Wild Rice and Chestnut Stuffing is the perfect addition to the Christmas goose.

Wild Rice and Chestnut Stuffing

2 tbsp butter or margarine

1 Granny Smith apple, peeled, cored and chopped

1 large celery stalk, diced

1 medium carrot, diced

1 small onion, diced

1/2 tsp salt

1/4 tsp pepper

1/4 tsp dried thyme leaves

2 14-oz cans chicken broth

1 4-oz pkg wild rice

1 cup parboiled rice

1 lb chestnuts

In a 3-quart saucepan melt 1 tbsp butter or margarine. Add the apple pieces and cook until softened. With a slotted spoon, remove the cooked apple to a small bowl; set aside. Add 1 tbsp butter to the same saucepan; melt butter and add celery, carrot, onion, salt, pepper and thyme. Cook until vegetables are tender-crisp and golden. Stir in chicken broth and wild rice. Over high heat, heat to boiling. Reduce heat to low, cover and simmer 35 minutes. Stir in 1 cup parboiled rice. Over high heat, heat to boiling. Reduce heat to low and simmer 25 minutes longer or until liquid is absorbed and white and wild rice are tender.

While rice is cooking prepare chestnuts. Cook chestnuts in a 4-quart saucepan in enough water to cover. Bring water to a boil, reduce heat to medium; cook 10 minutes. Remove the chestnuts 2 or 3 at a time to a cutting board; cut in half and scrape out the chestnut meat. When rice is cooked, stir in cooked apple and chestnut meat.

Roast Goose with Chestnut Stuffing

Remove giblets from the cavity. Wash goose inside and out. Drain well. Spoon Wild Rice and Chestnut Stuffing into the body cavity. Tie legs and tail together with string. Place goose breast-side up on a rack in a large roasting pan. Prick the skin in several places to drain fat during roasting. Rub salt and pepper over the goose. Roast goose in a 350°F oven for about 3 hours or until a meat thermometer, inserted into the thickest part of the meat, reaches 180°F. Place goose on a large platter. Let stand 10 minutes for easier carving.

In our house no Christmas dinner would be complete without an English Sherry Trifle. Although the recipe has changed slightly over the years, it is basically the same as when my mother and grandmother made it so many years ago.

English Sherry Trifle

2 eggs

1/8 tsp salt

1/4 cup sugar

1/2 cup half and half cream

1 1/2 tbsp cornstarch

2 tsp vanilla

1 lb pound cake

Raspberry or strawberry jam

3/4 cup dry sherry

1 large can fruit cocktail (drained, reserving 1 cup juice)

1 large pkg raspberry Jell-O

2 cups boiling water

1 cup whipping cream

2 tbsp sugar

Fresh raspberries

2 tbsp slivered almonds, toasted

In the top of a double boiler, beat eggs, salt and 1/4 cup sugar with a rotary beater until thoroughly blended. Add the cream and beat again. Dissolve cornstarch in a little of the liquid mixture, then add to the mixture. Add 1 tsp vanilla. Over boiling water, stir and cook until a soft custard consistency is reached. Set aside to cool. Cut pound cake into 3/4-inch slices and spread generously with raspberry or strawberry jam. Cut each slice into 3 rectangular fingers. Arrange the cake pieces in the bottom of a serving bowl. Pour the sherry over the pound cake and allow the cake to soak it up.

Open the can of fruit cocktail and drain the liquid, reserving 1 cup. Empty the Jell-O powder into a bowl and dissolve in 2 cups boiling water. Cool slightly and add fruit cocktail and reserved juice. Cool a bit more before pouring very slowly over the sherried pound cake. Refrigerate to set. When the Jell-O has set pour the cooled custard over it, cover with plastic wrap and refrigerate. Just before serving, whip cream with 2 tbsp sugar and remaining 1 tsp vanilla. Cover the custard with the whipped cream and garnish with fresh raspberries and toasted almonds.

Serves 12

The evergreens with snow are spread,
Drifts push up against the wall.
Each post wears a nightcap on its head,
Everything's dressed in the new snowfall.

—*Anonymous*

HANUKKAH, THE "FESTIVAL OF LIGHTS," is observed each year about this time. It celebrates the return of Jerusalem to the worship of God from Greek Syrian paganism in the year 165 B.C. This festival is possibly the most widely celebrated holiday in Jewish homes. Long before the Christian observance of Christmas, Hanukkah was an exciting and joyous time for Jewish children. For the modern Jewish person Hanukkah is much more than candlelighting, gifts for children and special meals. It is the knowledge and resolve that every human being—in every part of the world—must be free to worship in the way they choose.

Many years ago, when my husband George was alive, he arranged for a Jewish Rabbi and his family to come to our home during the time of Hanukkah. George felt that it was important for our daughters, who were brought up as Anglicans, to know and understand other faiths. We enjoyed a most delightful meal that included many traditional foods. I would like to share two of those with you now.

Sweet 'n' Sour Brisket

1 3–4 lb fresh beef brisket or boneless beef chuck pot roast
1/2 cup vinegar
1/2 cup apple juice
1/2 cup chili sauce
2 tbsp brown sugar
1 tsp salt
1/4 tsp pepper
2 medium onions, sliced
1 cup sliced celery with leaves
3 small cooking apples, cored and cut into wedges
2 tbsp cornstarch
1/4 cup cold water

Trim any fat from the meat and discard. In a small mixing bowl stir together vinegar, apple juice, chili sauce, brown sugar, salt and pepper until sugar and salt are dissolved. Place a large freezer bag in a large bowl. Place the meat in the bag; pour the marinade over the meat. Close the bag. Chill for 12–24 hours, turning the bag occasionally. Remove the meat from the bag, reserving the marinade. Place meat in a 3-quart casserole. Top with onions and celery. Pour the reserved marinade over meat and vegetables. Cover and roast in a 325°F oven about 3 hours or until the meat is very tender. Add the apples for the last 10 minutes. Remove meat, vegetables and apples to a serving platter (reserving juices), cover and keep warm.

For gravy, strain reserved juices, keeping 2 1/2 cups. In a medium saucepan stir cornstarch into 1/4 cup cold water. Add juices. Cook and stir over medium heat until slightly thickened. Cook and stir 2 more minutes.

Makes 10–12 servings

Potato Latkes with Applesauce

3 medium potatoes

3 lightly beaten eggs

1/2 cup all-purpose flour

1/2 cup shredded carrot

1/4 cup thinly sliced green onion

1/2 tsp salt

1/4 tsp garlic powder

1/4 tsp pepper

Vegetable oil for shallow frying

Peel potatoes and coarsely shred. Place shredded potato in cold water to prevent darkening. Drain well. Pat dry with paper towels. In a large mixing bowl stir together drained potatoes, eggs, flour, carrots, green onions, salt, garlic powder and pepper. In a 12-inch skillet heat 1 tbsp oil over medium heat. For each latke drop 1 slightly rounded tbsp of the potato mixture into the hot oil, spreading gently to about a 2 1/2-inch circle. Fry 4 or 5 at a time for 2–3 minutes or until the edges are crisp. Turn and fry 2–3 minutes more or until golden brown. Drain on paper towels; cover and keep warm. Repeat, adding oil as necessary. Serve with applesauce.

Makes 24

WHEN YOU KNOW THAT everyone is coming to your house over the holidays, it's nice to have a few special recipes that you can be sure will make any dinner extraordinary.

Stuffed Crown Roast of Pork makes a very elegant entrée for a large gathering.

Stuffed Crown Roast of Pork

1 tsp dried parsley flakes

3 tbsp all-purpose flour

1 plus 1/4 tsp dried thyme leaves

1/4 plus 1/4 tsp pepper

1 plus 3/4 tsp salt

1 7-lb pork rib crown roast

3 tbsp salad oil

l large onion, chopped

1 12-oz pkg mushrooms, coarsely chopped

3 stalks celery, chopped

6 cups (about 10 slices) firm white bread cubes

1/2 tsp chicken-flavoured instant bouillon

1/2 cup water

14 potatoes, peeled and quartered

In a small bowl mix dried parsley flakes, flour, 1 tsp dried thyme leaves and 1/4 tsp pepper. Rub inside and outside of pork rib crown roast with 1 tsp salt, then coat the outside with the flour mixture. Place roast, rib-ends down, in a large roasting pan. Roast in a 325°F oven for 2 hours.

Stuffing: In a 12-inch frypan over medium heat in 3 tbsp hot salad oil, cook onion until tender and golden, stirring occasionally. Over medium-high heat add mushrooms and celery, 3/4 tsp salt, 1/4 tsp dried thyme and 1/4 tsp pepper and cook until mushrooms are tender and golden and celery is tender-crisp. Stir in bread cubes, chicken bouillon and 1/2 cup water and toss until well mixed.

When pork has roasted 2 hours, remove from the oven and turn rib-ends up. Fill the cavity with stuffing. Insert a meat thermometer between 2 ribs into the thickest part of the meat. (Be sure that the point of the thermometer does not touch bone.) Place peeled potatoes around the roast and return to the oven. Continue roasting for about 1 1/2 hours more or until the thermometer reaches 170°F. (It takes about 30–35 minutes per pound total cooking time.) If the stuffing seems to be getting too brown, cover it with foil.

When the roast is done, place it on a warm platter. Let stand 15 minutes for easier carving. Remove potatoes from the pan. Keep warm in the oven (200°F). Meanwhile, prepare gravy using pan drippings (fat skimmed off), 3 tbsp flour, water, salt and pepper. Cook over medium heat, stirring constantly, until mixture boils and thickens slightly. To serve, arrange the roasted potatoes on a serving platter with the roast. Serve with gravy.

Makes 14 servings

DELICIOUS DESSERTS ARE A wonderful part of the festive season. To complement a rich dinner, Snow Creams with Raspberry Sauce are a light but eye-catching sensation.

Snow Creams with Raspberry Sauce

1 envelope unflavoured gelatin

1/2 cup water

2 cups heavy cream

1 1/3 cups superfine sugar

1 1/3 cups dairy sour cream

1 8-oz pkg cream cheese, softened

2 tsp vanilla

Raspberry Sauce:

1 10-oz pkg frozen unsweetened raspberries, thawed,
     or 2 cups fresh raspberries

1 1/4 tsp cornstarch

2/3 cup water

2/3 cup superfine sugar

3 tbsp red wine

1 1/3 cups heavy cream

Sprinkle gelatin over 1/2 cup water in a small cup; let stand 5 minutes to soften. Pour 2 cups heavy cream into a small saucepan. Bring to boiling. Remove from the heat, add gelatin, stir to dissolve. Stir in 1 1/3 cups superfine sugar. Transfer to a medium-size bowl. Cool. Add sour cream, cream cheese and vanilla to the cooled cream mixture. Beat until smooth. Pour into a serving bowl or 12 individual dessert dishes.

To prepare the Raspberry Sauce, place the raspberries in the container of a blender. Combine cornstarch with 2/3 cup water in a small bowl. Stir in the sugar. Add to the blender. Whirl until puréed. Strain into small saucepan. Heat over low heat, stirring constantly, until slightly thickened. Add red wine; chill.

To serve, beat the 1 1/3 cups heavy cream until stiff. Spoon 1 tbsp of the Raspberry Sauce over each serving of Snow Cream. Top with a dollop of whipped cream and a whole raspberry.

THIS TIME OF YEAR can be stressful if entertaining gets out of hand. Sometimes it's nice to have a few close friends over and have a variety of party "nibblers."

Stuffed Pumpernickel Loaf

*1 pkg fresh spinach, washed, then chopped (you may
      substitute 1 pkg frozen chopped spinach, thawed and
      squeezed to remove excess water)*

2 cups sour cream

1 cup mayonnaise (real, light or reduced fat)

1 pkg Knorr Vegetable Soup mix

1 can water chestnuts, drained and chopped

3 green onions, chopped

3/4 cup shredded cheddar cheese

1 large round pumpernickel, rye or sourdough bread

In a bowl combine spinach, sour cream, mayonnaise, soup
mix, water chestnuts and green onions. Mix well. Refrigerate
about 2 hours. Scoop out a large hollow through the top of the
bread loaf; fill with the dip. Sprinkle the cheese over the top
and serve with bread cubes cut from the bread taken from
the centre of the loaf. Be sure to have several sharp knives
on the serving tray so that the bread "shell" may be cut up
and eaten. Some people also serve assorted fresh vegetables
with the bread cubes as the dip is delicious with either.

Cheddar Cheese Dip

2 cups (1/2 lb) grated cheddar cheese

1/2 cup mayonnaise

1 can condensed cheese soup

1/4 tsp onion powder

1 tsp parsley flakes

1 tsp lemon juice

Combine ingredients and refrigerate in serving bowls until party time. Serve with crackers for dipping.

Holly Wreath Pizzas

1 pkg cheese pizza mix

1 jar pimiento-stuffed green olives

Use the packaged mix and make it into several small pizzas. After baking, decorate with sliced pimiento-stuffed green olives around the edges—pizzas will look like holly wreaths. Cut into small slices.

AS WE COME TO the end of this year I would like to wish you all "Happy Cooking" and leave you with one last recipe to enjoy.

Recipe for a Happy Family

1 1/2 cups politeness

3 cups love

4 tbsp willingness to work together

1 big dash unselfishness

2 cups pleasant disposition

1 cup happiness

1 1/2 tbsp encouragement

Season liberally with humour. Bake in an oven of warm contentment for the rest of your life.

Serves 6 big helpings with a smile

Index